A MARXIST STUDY OF SHAKESPEARE'S COMEDIES

A MARXIST STUDY OF SHAKESPEARE'S COMEDIES

Elliot Krieger

First published 1979 by
THE MACMILLAN PRESS LTD
London and Basingstoke
Associated companies in Delhi
Dublin Hong Kong Johannesburg Lagos
Melbourne New York Singapore Tokyo

Printed in Great Britain by
Unwin Brothers Ltd, Woking

British Library Cataloguing in Publication Data

Krieger, Elliot
 A Marxist study of Shakespeare's comedies
 1. Shakespeare, William — Comedies
 I. Title
 822.3'3   PR2981

 ISBN 0-333-26463-0

For Marge

Property was thus appalled,
That the self was not the same;
Single nature's double name
Neither two nor one was called.

SHAKESPEARE,
("The Phoenix and Turtle", 37–40)

Contents

Acknowledgements

All Shakespeare quotations are from *The Riverside Shakespeare*, textual editer G. Blakemore Evans (Boston, Houghton Mifflin Co., 1974).

An early version of Chapter 1 appeared in *The Minnesota Review*, (ns7, 1976); an early version of Chapter 5 appeared in *Zeitschrift für Anglistik und Amerikanistik* (Leipzig, 25:4, 1977).

Several friends read and commented on parts of the manuscript. I especially wish to thank Dick Fly, Irving Massey, Barry Phillips, and Bill Saunders for their helpful criticism.

My friend and colleague Max Bluestone read the entire manuscript with extraordinary care and attention. Without his criticism, the manuscript could not have become this book.

I do not know how to thank my wife, Marge Rooney, except to say that without her this book would not have been possible or worth while.

1 Introduction

"SINGLE NATURE'S DOUBLE NAME"

In each of Shakespeare's comedies one of two things happens. Either (a) the protagonists move from one location, in which the action begins, to another, in which it concludes, or (b) the action begins as a group of characters arrive in a new location. Critics refer to the location toward which the characters, hence the action, move as the "second world"; the location either in which the action begins or from which the characters have departed critics call the "primary world". The term "location" becomes inflated to "world" because in Shakespeare's comedies setting seems to have an active effect on the behavior and attitudes of the characters. Because the new location seems to exemplify and contain holiday, freedom, and harmony with nature, the second world itself, rather than what the characters do while there, seems to resolve the conflicts that had been established in the primary world.

Consequently, the second world differs fundamentally from the primary world, and critics have tried to understand the meaning of Shakespeare's comedies by emphasizing the distinction between the two worlds, by seeing the two worlds as alternatives. Sherman Hawkins, for example, writes that the drama "turns on the contrast between two worlds, two orders of experience, two perspectives on reality . . . the whole convention depends on the juxtaposition of two strongly contrasted locales, representing two different orders of reality".[1] To Clifford Leech, the two worlds "help to exhibit each other's shortcomings" and thereby demonstrate the "comparative goodness of what we may have".[2] The two worlds become separate and separable perspectives on each other, and on a "reality" found outside of both; the play becomes an expository essay using comparison and contrast. Each of the two worlds assumes a fixed position in relation to the static,

I

evaluative judgment of an audience that compares life in the primary with life in the second world.

I view the relation between the primary and second world in a different way. I see the primary and second world not as juxtaposed alternatives but as part of the same continuous representation of reality—single nature's double name. The second world develops from the contents of the primary world; specifically, the protagonists develop the second world as a strategy for living in the primary world. A process, therefore, connects the primary with the second world, as Harry Berger, Jr, makes clear when he describes the second world as:

> the playground, laboratory, theatre, or battlefield of the mind, a model or construct which the mind creates, a time or place which it clears, in order to withdraw from the actual environment. . . . It promises a clarified image of the world it replaces.[3]

Whereas Hawkins and Leech see both primary and second worlds as created by an author outside of each world, Berger tries to understand the second world as the result of an act of will made within a primary world. Berger's description of the second world allows us to see the second world as a strategy developed in response to the primary-world contents, as part of a process rather than as a polarity within a structure, an independent perspective, a separate reality.

Because of its emphasis on the creative faculty of "the mind", Berger's description frees us from restrictive ideas about dramatic space. The second world, that is, need not be a distinct spatial domain—a setting—into which the protagonists retreat. The second world is not defined solely as a new environment but as the protagonists' new or transformed attitude toward their environment; the second world depends upon a state of mind or of being, as when the same geographic environment can function as a second world of retreat for Rosalind and "everyday existence" for Corin. In fact, throughout Shakespeare's comedies characters who are living within a second world, a cleared space that shelters or separates them from the everyday concerns of time, conduct ongoing social exchanges with other characters—usually their servants, always their subordinates—who must maintain a continuous attention and responsibility to the everyday demands and restrictions of time, space, and degree. Because of this residual presence of primary-world consciousness throughout each of Shakespeare's comedies, we cannot rightly speak of an entire play as being transformed: each play contains within itself a second-world strategy; this strategy, however, transforms the initial situation of the play not through complete replacement of the primary world, but by separating those characters who can clear their own time or place from those who cannot.

Although dependent on a state of mind, the second world is not all *in* the mind. The desire to withdraw, the second-world attitude, develops as a second world only when the attitude is projected out *from* the mind, when consciousness acquires active material status in an environment. By means of retreat to a second world the mind engages itself with the environment, in that the protagonists in the second world circumscribe all of objective reality with their own subjectivity. As in a process of narcissistic regression, the mind that creates the second-world strategy abandons the external objects of its desire to "set the subject's own ego in their place". [4] This process enacted by the protagonists replaces, in a number of different ways, the objective and restrictive material conditions of the primary world. The second world generally replaces participation in work with participation in sport, play, or games: playing at being prince replaces the responsibility of actually being the prince; the hunt replaces the court. Further, in the second world ritual and ceremony replace the law, as, for example, the test of the caskets replaces Shylock's bond, or the fairy magic replaces the law of Athens. Perhaps most significant of all, the leisure of timelessness replaces measured clock time: Sir Toby can declare all time to be irrelevant, Rosalind can declare all time to be subjective, Olivia can use time only as a means to demarcate ritual, or Duke Theseus can use time to demarcate an interlude, during which clock time is to be ignored. Each of these replacements constitutes a freedom, and a distinctly personal one; each removes the protagonist from the matrix of social relations that imposes boundaries on the ego and its capabilities. Each replacement, in addition, removes the ego from history; although the development of a second world transforms the primary world, the second world itself—or in Berger's terms the "clarified image" that it "promises"—protects the protagonists from historical change, from transformation. Just as the emphasis on mind gets the protagonist out of the history of his or her body, away from the processes of maturation and decay, the asserted freedom from time within which the second world functions allows the protagonists to imagine that the world exists outside of history, as an "image". Freed from time, the protagonists can isolate and hold in place the forces of historical conflict—filial ingratitude, economic competition and instability, imperial or civil war; after these forces of historical change have been made static, they can be distinguished and distanced from the active and creative capacities of the protagonist's ego.

As the protagonists develop the second world, therefore, they also initiate a reversing effect: while the protagonists transform the environment into a manifestation of their subjective needs, they subordinate the autonomy of others who either live in or pass through their environment, they treat other subjects as if they were objects. Although the protagonists release their private fancy or vision from its limitations, the boundaries of the individual consciousness, and enact the fancy as a second world, a clarified image that determines social and historical relations, other people experience the second world as a restriction on their own autonomy. The transforming and regenerative effect of the second world that Berger's statement suggests can only apply with qualifications: at the same time that the protagonists experience the second world as a retreat, withdrawal, or replacement, others experience the second world as a domination, an exhibition of authority. Any character—Malvolio, for example—can abandon the actual environment in order to retreat to fantasy and abstraction. But only a protagonist who has social degree, and power, can develop a second world in which personal whims organize the social experience of others, in which the needs of the subject's ego replace the history of the primary world.

The development of a second world manifests aristocratic privilege: this is an idea so obvious that it has probably never been stated. But without stating the obvious we are liable to separate the second-world strategy from the material conditions, the specific class structure and social hierarchy, that make the strategy possible and successful. The second world does not emerge from a vacuum but from, and partially in response to, primary-world social conditions. When critics separate the second world from the primary-world social conditions, the second-world strategy appears to be a universal solution to the problems of the primary world. The second world then appears to produce an abstract moral condition such as "harmony" or "concord", beneficial to all of the characters save perhaps one or two (e.g. Jaques, Shylock, Malvolio) who may be excluded from the comic resolution for "balance". But the interests, needs, and fantasies of the different characters differ, and the differentiation has in part to do with social degree. Inasmuch as the second world develops from the primary-world social structure, the second-world strategy cannot lead to universal good: to the extent that the second world clarifies the subjective interests of the members of one social class, it is antagonistic to the interests of other classes. In implicitly denying that different social classes develop opposed interests, the idea of universal good is by its nature a revisionist fantasy, a way of interpreting and acknowledging only the comfortable and pro- gressive aspects of a given situation. Uncomfortable finding class struggle and class interests dramatized in Shakespeare's comedies, many critics abstract the concrete motives, solutions, and themes of the plays from the particular class interests that these qualities serve; many critics place the comedies on the refined level of the universals of human nature, within which the class interests are absorbed and obscured. These critics argue that the plays articulate "neutral" themes such as "love's truth", the value of the imagination, or the need for mercy. They see that the clarified image reveals a world of holiday leisure, but they do not see that without servants, no leisure time would be available for the protagonists. They see that the plays celebrate hierarchy in society and correspondence between nature and society, but they do not see that those who formulate the celebration correspond only to the highest level of nature. They see that the second world enables the protagonists to discover their true identities and to assert their autonomy, but they do not see that others must discover their "true identity" by abandoning autonomy and devoting them- selves to service. These critics, in short, find universal truths rather than class interests in Shakespeare's comedies. And their partial, censored interpretations conform to aristocratic needs and fan- tasies. In this study I hope to counter this "censorship"; I will try to understand what the second world does, how it argues for and against, whom it includes and excludes.

The clarified image that the second world reveals serves the interests of the ruling-class protagonists—for they develop the second world—and opposes the interests of other classes. The clarified image serves these ruling class interests in part by creating the illusion that ruling-class interests do not exist—more specifically, that the protagonists seek only harmony and concord, universal good. Harmony and concord, however, originate not as universal truths but as aspects of aristocratic needs and fantasies. When seen in terms of aristocratic needs, the abstractions harmony and concord become rephrased and translated into social policy: hierarchy and stability. By restoring abstractions to the concrete level of social-class relations, critics can identify seemingly universal notions with the class interests out of which they develop and which they serve.

Because it creates the illusion that class interests are universal interests, the second world functions as an ideological system. As the second worlds differ somewhat in each of Shakespeare's comedies, the exact contents of each ideological system differ somewhat. Each ideological system, however, hides from view the elements of class struggle. The second worlds hide class struggle in several ways: sometimes crudely, during only a moment of the play, as when a servant (Adam in *As You Like It*, for example) endorses the aristocratic ideal of a static social hierarchy; sometimes subtly, as when the form of the drama itself usurps the potential opposition between classes. In *The Merchant of Venice*, for example, the double-world form absorbs a class struggle within the contents: the form would make us feel as though the retreat to Belmont embodies such a perfect realization of harmonic correspondences that the forces of bourgeois opposition will vanish as if by magic.

But we should not isolate the second-world ideological system from the form of the whole comedy. The play itself both produces and contains the second world and its ideology; the ideology does not circumscribe the entire play. The ideology, therefore, has a *place* within the comedy, and should not subsume the meaning of the comedy as a whole. Rather than expressing a ruling-class ideology, Shakespeare's comedies examine the process through which a class creates its ideology. These plays explore the strategies that the aristocrats adopt in order to identify their interests with universal interests and with nature.

Finally, however, and at a point somewhere beyond the plays I consider here, the form of the comedies becomes its own undoing, or at least it undoes the aristocratic ideologies contained within the second worlds. The form of the comedies, when thought of as a process, moves not simply in a straight line, from primary world to second world, but also backwards and upwards. The comedies move backwards in that the second world develops as an antithesis to the primary-world social conditions, and thus the second world transforms, reverses, or negates the primary-world contents (the economy of Venice, the law of Athens, the tyranny of the court) with which the play began. The comedies move upwards as well, in that the conclusions, often through the use of magic and theistic intervention, proclaim that the second world has transcended the primary-world contents. In other words, unlike a linear model, according to which the primary-world conditions would remain, in effect, "still there", the protagonists merely having moved on to a new location, Shakespeare's comedies actually re-place the primary-world contents: the second world transforms rather than leaves behind the primary world and therefore the primary world no longer exists as such. The dramatic form of the comedies, which I will call dialectical, negates the second-world ideology. While the ideology within the play states that static hierarchies and ordered structures constitute and determine a social ideal, the form of the play demonstrates that material conditions can be transformed, replaced, or negated by human action. In this regard the dialectical dramatic form negates the static ideology that the protagonists express through the dramatic contents. To understand Shakespeare's plays and his sense of social class, we must understand how his plays both express and negate an ideology, we must begin to analyze the dialectics of Shakespeare's comedies.

2 *The Merchant of Venice*

"A MUTUAL STAND" *Belmont*

The Merchant of Venice Act V includes such leisurely, con-
templative passages as:

> Here will we sit, and let the sounds of music
> Creep in our ears. Soft stillness and the night
> Become the touches of sweet harmony.
> Sit, Jessica. Look how the floor of heaven
> Is thick inlaid with patens of bright gold.
> There's not the smallest orb which thou behold'st
> But in his motion like an angel sings,
> Still quiring to the young-ey'd cherubins;
> Such harmony is in immortal souls,
> But whilst this muddy vesture of decay
> Doth grossly close it in, we cannot hear it, (V. i. 55–65)

and:

> . . . do but note a wild and wanton herd
> Or race of youthful and unhandled colts,
> Fetching mad bounds, bellowing and neighing loud,
> Which is the hot condition of their blood,
> If they but hear perchance a trumpet sound,
> Or any air of music touch their ears,
> You shall perceive them make a mutual stand,
> Their savage eyes turn'd to a modest gaze,
> By the sweet power of music; therefore the poet
> Did feign that Orpheus drew trees, stones, and floods;
> Since nought so stockish, hard, and full of rage,
> But music for the time doth change his nature.
> The man that hath no music in himself,
> Nor is not moved with concord of sweet sounds,
> Is fit for treasons, strategems, and spoils . . . (71–85)

These passages, both indirectly and directly, help establish the atmosphere of Belmont. They do so indirectly in that as casual, uninterrupted monologues each lengthy speech suggests an environment wherein people can use time at leisure, can fill time with language. The passages more directly create an atmosphere for Belmont by describing a neoPlatonic cosmology, by painting a so-called "Elizabethan World Picture", in which the universe coheres because of a harmonic relation among its parts. The two passages make this harmonic world-view into a context for Belmont; they place Belmont at the very centre of the imagined cosmology. Belmont becomes an earthly reference point at the centre of a system of concentric spheres that create harmonic music by their "motion". This music of the spheres binds together, within a hierarchy, all of nature, the whole chain of being: the angels (61), cherubins (62), the "immortal souls" of human beings (63), animals (71ff.), vegetables (80), and minerals (80). Human beings, unique within the hierarchy, both contain and are contained by the hierarchic system: the harmony in immortal souls makes human beings microcosmic representations of the entire cosmic system, and the same harmony binds human beings to their place within the system. Harmonic principles, in a sense, arrange and order the cosmos and they make each element within the cosmos content by nature with its determined position. Harmony gives natural sanction to the principle of hierarchy.

This view of the world, in which an abstract and immaterial heavenly harmony determines and arranges the chain of being, directly replaces the world-view that has, up to Act V, formed the predominant context or background for Belmont. The heavenly harmony, in effect, replaces the bourgeois world of Venice. In Venice, possession of material substances, of gold, determines one's position within the social order. The Belmont atmosphere emerges or gets articulated in part so as to contradict the Venetian materialism. The two atmospheric passages quoted above presuppose a complete idealism; each argues that "the mind was nothing else but a kind of harmony".[1] In fact, whereas Venice characteristically conjoins the human body with material wealth—"I would my daughter were dead at my foot, and the jewels in her ear!" (II. i. 87–9)—Belmont associates the body, notably the ear, with the immateriality of musical harmony:

> Here will we sit, and let the sounds of music
> Creep in our ears,

and:

> With sweetest touches pierce your mistress' ear. (67)

To understand the meaning or cause of this shift in imagery from jewels to music, from material to ideal, we must see the Belmont world-view as the end point in a dramatic process, we must place the Belmont world-view within the social context from which it emerges: we must consider what the particular emphasis on harmony accomplishes, and for whom.

Above all, the emphasis on harmony, especially through its association with heavenly hierarchies and the chain of being, protects the social position of the ruling class. By attributing the arrangement of the social structure to an immaterial force outside of human action and control, the belief in harmony articulates the fantasy that nature—or heaven—itself sanctions and determines the extant class structure. Whereas according to a materialist world-view one's class status depends on one's accumulated wealth, according to the idealist world-view articulated in Belmont the harmony within one's soul determines one's social position. Although superficially the Belmont idealism sounds the more democratic, in practice the idealistic system more effectively fixes the social structure and protects those at its apex, for it implies that even if a man becomes wealthy he cannot really change his true class status, his position within the harmonic structure. The harmonic system protects the aristocracy from the economic conditions of the material world, conditions that threaten their social status; by creating a separation between material wealth and one's harmony with nature, the idealist system allows one to be economically poor but still, by nature, an aristocrat. Conversely, faith in a fixed, harmonic social order leads to the criticism of social upstarts, as in this speech by the Prince of Aragon:

> O that estates, degrees, and offices
> Were not deriv'd corruptly, and that clear honor
> Were purchas'd by the merit of the wearer!
> How many then should cover that stand bare?

How many be commanded that command?
How much low peasantry would then be gleaned
From the true seed of honor? and how much honor
Pick'd from the chaff and ruin of the times
To be new varnish'd? (II. ix. 41–9)

The insistence that social status should depend on inheritance, on a quality of nature—"the true seed"—rather than on human achievement, in effect allows the aristocracy to determine its own boundaries or criteria: estates, degrees, and offices do not automatically make one an aristocrat, nor have those ruined by "the times" necessarily lost their true aristocratic status.

By freeing class status from the fluctuations of fortune this idealistic, harmonic world-view makes the aristocratic social position permanent and secure. The harmonic world-view removes class status from the referent of wealth, from determination within the material world, and it assumes that a context outside of society itself determines the class relationships within society. Paradoxically, though, this dependence on an external concept, on harmony, as the determinant of class relationships makes it impossible to determine in isolation the worth or stature of any individual. Within the materialism of Venice, worth correlates with wealth; within Belmont, where worth depends on a harmony among elements, one cannot be measured or evaluated except in regard to others. Portia's observations on the relative nature of beauty qualify and explain the heavenly harmonies enunciated and celebrated earlier:

A substitute shines brightly as a king
Until a king be by
· · ·
Nothing is good, I see, without respect
· · ·
The crow doth sing as sweetly as the lark
When neither is attended; and I think
The nightingale, if she should sing by day
When every goose is cackling, would be thought
No better a musician than the wren.
How many things by season season'd are
To their right praise and true perfection! (V. i. 94–108)

This sense of perspectives neatly circumscribes and completes the aristocratic world-view, or ideology, developed in Belmont. Perspectives extend into the social structure the belief that the harmony within one's soul corresponds to a heavenly harmony; now one's harmonic position, one's relative goodness, depends not only on one's accordance with an external, heavenly harmony but also on one's relation to those above and below one's self within the social scale. One must maintain or create a harmony on earth by finding a correct, harmonic position with "respect" to others. Further, by bringing the heavenly harmonies, in a sense, down to earth, the aristocracy can explain away its suppression or subordination of other social classes: one must subordinate others to establish one's own goodness, for nothing is good or bad without respect, and, additionally, those placed in a subordinate position have not been made "bad" in any absolute sense, since they, too, can find "their right praise and true perfection" with respect to others whom *they* can subordinate.

The aristocratic ideology thus combines in one system an absolute definition of moral goodness with a complete moral relativism. Because it unites these antithetic moralities, the aristocratic world-view can produce such apparently contradictory statements as Bassanio's "So may the outward shows be least themselves—/The world is still deceiv'd with ornament", (III. ii. 73—4) and Portia's judgmental dismissal of the Prince of Morocco, "Let all of his complexion choose me so", (II. vii. 79); more profoundly, the same ideology can lead both to Portia's "The quality of mercy is not strain'd", (IV. i. 184) and to her "Down therefore, and beg mercy of the Duke", (363). In each case the latter statement merely brings the aesthetic or moral absolute down to the earthly and therefore relative social condition: the Prince of Morocco is perfectly "good", for he has his own internal harmony, in the abstract, out of context. But within society, with respect to Portia's goodness, he is found lacking. Similarly, in the abstract, mercy dropping "as the gentle rain from heaven" (185), forms part of a universal harmony. But within the social system of relative moral values, the Christian moral position can be so "good" with "respect" to Shylock that Portia need not show mercy in order to attain her "right praise and true perfection". The respective morality, the relativism, allows the aristocracy to maintain its superiority to or authority over others, while the asserted absolute standards of moral and aesthetic judgement allow it to identify its maintained superiority with universal principles of harmony in and correspondence to a natural or a cosmological hierarchy.

The aristocratic ideology contrasts with the far simpler moral system of Venice, where to be "a good man" is to be "sufficient". The Venetian system may at first appear crass and inhuman, but it has positive qualities as well, such as legal, if not social, egalitarianism. "The Duke cannot deny the course of law" (III. iii. 26) although he detests Shylock ("A stony adversary, an inhuman wretch, / Uncapable of pity, void and empty / From any dram of mercy", IV. i. 4–6) and publicly ridicules him ("We all expect a gentle answer, Jew!", 34). Venice has more intense biases and prejudices than Belmont, but, until Portia intervenes, the course of law, an external system of social harmony, completely oblivious of the particular moral qualities of the individuals before it, governs the fate of the characters. The laws of Venice can side with Shylock against the "good" Antonio. In effect, then, wealth determines goodness in Venice because morality has been superceded by legality; that is, the court of law has no interest in who is good, who is bad—only in who is legally correct. Similarly, the Rialto has no interest in relative goodness, only in relative wealth.

People in Venice, consequently, become devoid of qualities, or they retain only mannerisms and eccentricities, qualities having nothing to do with their sense of self and public goodness, or, in commercial terms, worth. Since the Venetian moral system depends on external qualities, on the attachments and appendages of wealth, Venetians can engage in business with those whose internal, personal qualities they detest. In fact, Shylock enunciates the moral distinction that governs all segments of Venetian society when he says to Bassanio:

> I will buy with you, sell with you, talk with you, walk with you, and so following; but I will not eat with you, drink with you, nor pray with you. What news on the Rialto? (I. iii. 35–8)

We see a distinction operating here between public commerce and private habits and values: commercial acquisition in Venice serves the same function as the harmonic system in Belmont; it is analogous with the heavenly harmony according to which those in

Belmont find their place with respect to one another. Possession of external objects thus makes it unnecessary to observe inner qualities; people have their "goodness" and their place within the Venetian social system determined solely with respect to what they own.

In Venice, then, the relation between persons and the objects of the environment is one of potential possession, of purchasing; this becomes apparent at the very beginning of the play, as Salerio and Salanio, subordinate, to the processes of commerce, nature:

> . . . had I such venture forth,
> The better part of my affections would
> Be with my hopes abroad. I should be still
> Plucking the grass to know where sits the wind,

food:

> My wind cooling my broth
> Would blow me to an ague when I thought
> What harm a wind too great might do at sea,

time:

> I should not see the sandy hour-glass run
> But I should think of shallows and of flats,

and religion:

> Should I go to church
> And see the holy edifice of stone,
> And not bethink me straight of dangerous rocks . . . ?
> (I. i. 15−31)

This subordination, which also serves to elevate the social value of possession, continues to operate throughout the Venetian segments of the play, reaching a climax in Shylock's vituperative outburst during the trial:

> You have among you many a purchas'd slave,
> Which like your asses, and your dogs and mules,

> You use in abject and in slavish parts,
> Because you bought them. Shall I say to you,
> "Let them be free! Marry them to your heirs!
> Why sweat they under burdens? Let their beds
> Be made as soft as yours, and let their palates
> Be season'd with such viands"? You will answer,
> "The slaves are ours." (IV. i. 90—8)

Shylock extends to its logical extreme the commercial morality postulated by Salerio and Salanio, and by implicitly accepting slavery as part of the economic system, he proposes that economic forces should subordinate freedom. Shylock's system assumes that the extreme social divisions, the oppositions among classes of people, result from purchasing power, the process of acquisition; in this he of course directly opposes the aristocratic ideology, in which social degree reflects and makes manifest heavenly harmony and hierarchy.

Ownership in Belmont, according to the aristocratic ideology, derives not from purchase but from right: internal qualities, not the external function of commercial acquisition, determine relations among classes and between people and the material objects of the environment. This aristocratic concept of ownership by natural right contains an implicit nostalgia for the past and a contempt for the new order of things; the archetypical aristocrat, Aragon, assumes that "the merit of the wearer" should purchase "clear honor" and thereby secure the social elevation and racial purity of his class (II. ix. 39—49). About to choose the leaden casket, Bassanio adopts a similar attitude without the explicit class bias, scorning that which is "purchas'd by the weight", (III. ii. 89). Like Aragon, Portia herself, although whimsically, clearly expresses the aristocratic attitude toward possession, with her glancing reference to the anachronistic aspects of aristocratic idealism:

> O, these naughty times
> Puts bars between the owners and their rights!
> (III. ii. 18—19)

These "bars" can represent any of a number of things, but most obviously they represent the mediating and, to an extent, egalitarian, function of money. Portia implicitly assumes that those who own have a right to own; the "bars" refer to the acts of acquisition needed to certify ownership. Purchasing, therefore, conflicts with itself: in one sense it reduces all members of society to equal stature, making distinction among people only according to what external things they can acquire and therefore, at least in theory, making "honor" equally accessible to all; at the same time, however, purchasing adds the external, the legal, sanction to the extant system of class relations, allowing the continuation of a very unharmonic "use" of one class by another because the slaves, "like your asses, and your dogs and mules", are "purchas'd".

The two different forms of ownership, by purchasing and by right, derive from the two opposed moral systems of the play. From the Venetian moral standpoint one has a "right" to purchase slaves only in that one has the money to do so; no qualitative and natural differentiation, but only the economic relation of purchaser to purchased, separates one class or role from the other. The Belmont moral system, in which one owns or should own by "rights", presupposes that the owner/slave or master/servant relation accords with a cosmological harmony, that the harmony within each immortal soul determines each individual's fixed position within the social harmony. Further, according to the relativism contained within the Belmont moral system, the social position of those owned is neither good nor bad in itself, for one can measure such qualities only with "respect" to the social position of others. Among themselves, therefore, those owned can attain their own right praise and true perfection, a relative autonomy. In this sense, then, the system of ownership by rights allows the Belmont aristocracy to avoid the moral responsibility for the ownership of others that remains implicit within the Venetian system: those who purchase slaves acknowledge that their money allows them to objectify and to "use" others as property. Those who claim to own by rights, however, imagine that their ownership of others helps to maintain the stability and the harmony of an entire social order.

"I GIVE THEM WITH THIS RING" *Property*

The sequence of exchanges of Portia's (and of Nerissa's) wedding ring enacts the distinction between the aristocratic and the bourgeois modes of ownership. Shakespeare uses the ring in *The Merchant of Venice* as a symbol, an *objective* symbol, for the social exchanges that occur in the play: while itself remaining intact, the circumstantial use of the object changes with changed conditions, thereby allowing us to measure and compare two opposed attitudes toward property and possession.[2]

Portia's ring is first exchanged in Belmont; Portia uses the ring to indicate her complete surrender of herself and of all she owns and controls to Bassanio:

> her gentle spirit
> Commits itself to yours to be directed,
> As from her lord, her governor, her king.
> Myself, and what is mine, to you and yours
> Is now converted. But now I was the lord
> Of this fair mansion, master of my servants,
> Queen o'er myself; and even now, but now,
> This house, these servants, and this same myself
> Are yours—my lord's!—I give them with this ring,
> Which when you part from, lose, or give away,
> Let it presage the ruin of your love,
> And be my vantage to exclaim on you. (III. ii. 163–74)

The ring, in this exchange, although a piece of property, primarily functions as a symbol or token: it represents a complete transferral of all property, or, to adopt Portia's phrasing, a "conversion". Explicitly, Portia refers to two kinds of conversions, an economic or commercial and a social: the property itself, including Portia's servants, exchanges masters (a process prefigured by Launcelot's shift of allegiances), whereas Portia is converted from master into servant. This emphasizes the completion and the totality of the exchange, in that her handing the ring over signifies more than just a transfer of property: it indicates a change in the nature of things.

Bassanio's prelude to Portia's offer of herself and all she owns helps establish the context within which the ring exchange begins and, more significantly, from which it departs. Bassanio initiates a series of commercial metaphors as he leaves the leaden casket and approaches Portia—"I come by note, to give and to receive", (140) "until confirm'd, sign'd, ratified by you", (148)—a motif that Portia adopts:

>   That only to stand high in your account,
>   I might in virtues, beauties, livings, friends,
>   Exceed account. But the full sum of me
>   Is sum of something; which, to term in gross . . .
>   (III. ii. 155—8)

Portia even embellishes the commercial motif with her quantified references to abstract qualities: "I would be trebled twenty times myself, /A thousand times more fair, ten thousand times more rich", (153—4). But the exchange signified by the bestowal of the ring goes beyond these specific enumerated and material qualities; the exchange becomes a coalescence and inversion of spirit, as emphasized in Portia's conclusive remark, and attains a mystical and prophetic aspect. Bassanio responds to Portia's gift appropriately: he, too, relinquishes the commercial references with which he had initiated the public exchange, and he appropriates Portia's references to himself as "her governor, her king":

>   And there is such confusion in my powers,
>   As after some oration fairly spoke
>   By a beloved prince, there doth appear
>   Among the buzzing pleased multitude,
>   Where every something, being blent together,
>   Turns to a wild of nothing, save of joy
>   Express'd and not express'd. But when this ring
>   Parts from this finger, then parts life from hence;
>   O then be bold to say Bassanio's dead! (III. ii. 177—85)

Before the exchange of the ring, Bassanio imagined himself "hearing applause and universal shout, /Giddy in spirit" and "doubtful whether what I see be true", and he explained his confusion by comparing himself to "one of two contending in a prize" (III. ii. 143—4, 147, 141); after the exchange he explains that his confusion results from his being, in a sense, *above* the battle.

Bassanio's acceptance of the ring incorporates and confirms the absolute quality of the exchange that Portia proposes; his shift in imagery indicates the change in his nature, the change in his relation to his environment. His identification of his own life with his possession of the ring further emphasizes the spiritual quality of the exchange and the ritual value of the ring. It is important that the ring has become more than a piece of property or even an indication of the possession of property; Bassanio accepts the ring as a token of the unification of flesh with spirit and as an indication of his newly predominant position in society, of his superiority to the contractual, enumerative qualities of objective material possession. Possession of the ring confirms Bassanio's lordship over Portia and thereby his "right" to ownership of Portia and all she had owned or controlled; without the attendant avowals of change in nature and the mystical associations, the ring would have merely certified the contract, the "purchase" of Portia, toward which the initial commercial images of the betrothal scene seemed to have been leading.

When the ring is re-exchanged in Venice after the completion of the trial, the commercial value of the property is restored, or, rather, the ring re-assumes its place as a piece of property. After the Duke departs from the court asking (telling?) Antonio to "gratify" the disguised Portia, Bassanio offers her the "three thousand ducats, due unto the Jew", (IV. i. 411). Portia magnanimously refuses the offer, claiming to be "well satisfied" and thereby "well paid": "My mind was never yet more mercenary", (415–18). (It is, of course, her own three thousand ducats that she can refuse so magnanimously.) But Portia does relent, and agrees to "take some remembrance . . . as a tribute, /Not as fee," (422–3). She selects, with a touch of malice ("Do not draw back your hand, I'll take no more, /And you in love shall not deny me this!," 428–9), Bassanio's ring. The ring then becomes the subject of an evaluative discussion: Bassanio plays down the exchange value of the ring ("This ring, good sir, alas, it is a trifle!", 430) and emphasizes the private, ceremonial value the ring has for him alone:

> Good sir, this ring was given me by my wife,
> And when she put it on, she made me vow
> That I should neither sell, nor give, nor lose it.
> (IV. i. 441–3)

Portia peevishly responds ("That 'scuse serves many men to save their gifts", 444) and departs, probably in secret pleased with Bassanio's fidelity to his wedding vow.[3]

But after Portia has departed, Antonio pleads with Bassanio:

> My Lord Bassanio, let him have the ring.
> Let his deservings and my love withal
> Be valued 'gainst your wive's commandement.
>
> (IV. i. 449–51)[4]

In succeeding, Antonio's plea proposes and enacts a different—the commercial, Venetian—attitude toward ownership, an attitude to which Bassanio temporarily acquiesces. Antonio sees the ring as something to which Bassanio can attach a value; moreover, Antonio goes so far as to suggest that abstract qualities inherent in human behavior and affection—his deservings, my love, your wive's commandement—can likewise be "valued 'gainst" one another. These are the public, material attitudes of Venice, the counterparts of Shylock's calculations and measurements; Antonio's bourgeois sense of ownership reduces all qualities to the common denominator of "value" and effects a system of distribution, of bestowal and purchase, based on the relative levels of supply and of need. Confronted with the Venetian public assessment of value, Bassanio relinquishes, along with the ring, his private and ideal relation to property, his faith that the ring signifies and guarantees his lordly dominance of his environment.

When Portia's ring is restored to Bassanio, this time framed and thereby intensified by the parallel episode of Nerissa's ring, the exchange once more clarifies and reverses the opposition between the ring as material possession used in payment of a fee (Gratiano says that the clerk had "begg'd" the ring "as a fee", (V. i. 164) even though Bassanio had earlier offered Portia "some re-membrance" explicitly "as a tribute, / Not as fee") and as a token of a spiritual ceremony of bondage and transformation. Gratiano tries to excuse his giving of Nerissa's ring by arguing that the ring had no great material value—"a hoop of gold, a paltry ring," (148)—but Nerissa removes Gratiano from the commercial terms of the argument:

> What talk you of the posy or the value?
> You swore to me, when I did give [it] you,
> That you would wear it till your hour of death.
>
> (V. i. 151–3)

That is, Nerissa argues that the value of the ring entirely depends on the moral and symbolic circumstances in which it was bestowed, that it has ideal rather than material value. Portia reinforces this distinction; for her, the ring—"riveted with faith unto your flesh", (169)—should not be exchanged "for the wealth /That the world masters", (173—4).

This scene develops the opposition between the relative and the absolute attitudes toward possession so as to emphasize the contextual influences on Bassanio's decision to surrender the ring. Unlike Gratiano, Bassanio avoids referring to the relative value of the ring itself as he defends his action; he instead tries to delineate the circumstantial conditions under which he acted: "to whom", "for whom", "for what", and "how unwillingly" he "gave" or "left" the ring (193—6), and, further:

> What should I say, sweet lady?
> I was enforc'd to send it after him,
> I was beset with shame and courtesy,
> My honor would not let ingratitude
> So much besmear it. (V. i. 215—19)

Bassanio refers to his action as "this enforced wrong", (240). Portia's attitude toward possession, and toward honour, does not, however, depend on the pressures of social conditions; for her, the value of the ring derives from a holistic interpretation of "the virtue of the ring, / . . . her worthiness that gave the ring, /Or your own honor to contain the ring", (199—201) which can be neither altered nor compared with an intervening social demand. Consequently, Portia must return the ring—"the thing held as a ceremony" (206)—through a recapitulation of the ceremonial process. She uses the restoration to extract once more an oath "by my soul" (pointedly not a commercial "oath of credit" 246) of faith from Bassanio (247—8), and, interestingly, once more to bind Antonio, this time upon forfeit of his soul, not his body, and to her, not to the Venetian economic and legal system:

> . . . . I dare be bound again,
> My soul upon the forfeit, that your lord
> Will never more break faith advisedly.

Portia. Then you shall be his surety. Give him this . . .
> (V. i. 251—4)

In returning the ring by binding Bassanio's and Antonio's souls, Portia has accomplished several significant tasks. First, she has restored the ring to its initial position as symbolic token, removing its tainted nature as something begged for a fee, one object that can be valued against others. Second, Portia has elevated her own position vis-à-vis her husband, using the ring to inform him "objectively" of her role at the trial. When Portia bestowed the ring initially, she did so as an act of self-subordination; she had reduced her "gentle spirit" into an object contained within the environment to be dominated by Bassanio: "This house, these servants, and this same myself /Are yours—my lord's"! With the restoration, Portia emerges from the environment into a renewed position of dominance, an elevated position from which she can ceremoniously, and with a self-conscious metaphorical hint of mysticism and deism, redistribute the commercial wealth of Venice, "drop manna in the way /Of starved people", (294– 5).

Finally, Portia articulates the aristocratic attitude toward wealth. Almost all of the dramatic conflict in the Venetian sections of the play concerns the difficulties associated with the acquisition and conveyance of wealth; Portia's action concludes *The Merchant of Venice* with the sense that wealth falls from the sky, appears without warning:

> Unseal this letter soon;
> There you shall find that three of your argosies
> Are richly come to harbor suddenly.
> You shall not know by what strange accident
> I chanced on this letter. (V. i. 275–9)

Here we see an extreme version of the antithesis to the "bars between the owners and their rights"; the rituals of exchange enacted at the conclusion of *The Merchant of Venice*, which propose a ceremonial relation between people and their material possessions, redefine wealth as a quality rather than an appendage, assure that one's degree of wealth will correspond to one's poise, generosity, and faith in the social order.

"AND FROM YOUR LOVE I HAVE A WARRANTY"
Thriving

The characters' treatment and exchange of material objects enacts
two opposed attitudes toward property in *The Merchant of Venice*;
the opposition between property as something purchased and
property as something owned by "rights" shades over into a
different kind of opposition, that between two views of one's place
within the established social order. This latter opposition never
gets objectified in the same way that opposed attitudes toward
possession become located in the rings; rather, the opposition
remains objectively diffuse and finds its primary expression in the
language of moral sentiment. In essence, the aristocratic largesse,
the willingness to give and hazard all, characteristic primarily of
Bassanio and, on the other side, the bourgeois closed system of
restraint and retention—"fast bind, fast find", (II. v. 54)— characteristic of Shylock express the opposing views regarding one's
place in the social order.

Many readers have isolated this opposition as the central moral
contrast of the play, arguing that true participation in "love's
wealth" can only come to those with immediate generosity such as
Bassanio's:

Gratiano: I have a suit to you.
Bassanio: You have obtain'd it, (II. ii. 177)

that those who use, give, or venture their wealth will "questionless
be fortunate", (I. i. 176). As C. L. Barber writes, "the whole play
dramatizes the conflict between the mechanisms of wealth and the
masterful, social use of it".[5] To this we might say, with Portia,
"good sentences, and well pronounc'd", (I. ii. 10) but utterly
meaningless outside of the class context in which the play develops
them. The initial difference at least between Shylock's and
Bassanio's "thrift" and degree of generosity should be obvious:
Shylock's "well-won thrift" is his own, is earned (I. iii. 50),
whereas Bassanio's is borrowed, and, in a sense, in the mind: "I
have a mind presages me such thrift", (I. i. 175). Bassanio, that is,
thrives because he thinks that he should and convinces others that
he will: he precisely illustrates the social application of aristocratic

credit, the financial success that follows fast upon social belonging. The bourgeois social status of Shylock ("you take my life /When you do take the means whereby I live", IV. i. 376— 7) and of Antonio ("Sweet lady, you have given me life and living, /For here I read for certain that my ships /Are safely come to road", V. i. 286— 8) derives directly from their degree of wealth and of credit; Bassanio's wealth and credit, conversely, derives directly from his aristocratic status, completely independent of his own financial means:

> To you, Antonio,
> I owe the most in money and in love,
> And from your love I have a warranty
> To unburthen all my plots and purposes .
> How to get clear of all the debts I owe.
> (I. i. 130—4)

Bassanio embodies the aristocratic attitude toward wealth: his wealth derives from the love others bear him, and, as such, wealth becomes for him something organic and inexhaustible, correspondent to his position in Venetian society. He believes that to recover money one must waste more money, just as he would risk losing a second arrow in order to recover a first one (I. i. 139— 52); he lacks Gratiano's ominous sense of the loss potential with adventuring forth:

> How like a younger or a prodigal
> The scarfed bark puts from her native bay,
> Hugg'd and embraced by the strumpet wind!
> How like the prodigal doth she return,
> With over-weather'd ribs and ragged sails,
> Lean, rent, and beggar'd by the strumpet wind!
> (II. vi. 14— 19)

Bassanio's generosity, then, derives from his aristocratic assumption that wealth does not depend on current material possessions, or, put another way, that his social position assures unlimited credit. The second world of Belmont isolates and exaggerates these assumptions by temporarily removing them from their material base. While in Venice, Bassanio always had,

quite literally, to draw his unlimited personal credit with Antonio
from Antonio's economically determined credit, "where money
is", (I. i. 184): the two forms of credit were, especially from
Antonio's point of view, interdependent. The retreat to Belmont,
in large part, frees Bassanio from this interdependence; nearly the
first words we hear in Belmont inform us of the surfeit of Portia's
world, and contrast with the Venetian scarcity (I. ii. 3–9).
Whereas Belmont seems to be a world of multiplication:

> Portia: I would be trebled twenty times myself,
> A thousand times more fair, ten thousand times more
> rich, (III. ii. 154–5)

and:

> Portia: What sum owes he the Jew?
> Bassanio: For me, three thousand ducats.
> Portia: What, no more?
> Pay him six thousand, and deface the bond;
> Double six thousand, and then treble that . . .;
>   (III. ii. 297–300)

Venice, in a sense, is a world of division:

> My ventures are not in one bottom trusted,
> Nor to one place; nor is my whole estate
> Upon the fortune of this present year, (I. i. 42–4)

and:

> he hath an argosy bound to Tripolis, another to the Indies; I
> understand moreover upon the Rialto, he hath a third at
> Mexico, a fourth for England, and other ventures he hath
> squand'red abroad, (I. iii. 18–21)

and:

> If every ducat in six thousand ducats
> Were in six parts, and every part a ducat,
> I would not draw them . . . (IV. i. 85–9)

The Venetians divide their fortunes specifically so as to avoid the risk of losing everything at once; to be incorporated into Belmont one must, in a single action, "give and hazard all he hath". These two rudimentary moral systems are not diametric opposites, however, but are antithetic terms within a single dialectical system.

To understand the interdependence of the supposedly opposite moralities we must distinguish between the aristocratic fantasies of unlimited, organic wealth and the material base of wealth as correspondent to a specific and limited supply of capital. When Antonio and the exchange system of the Rialto intrude upon the ritualized exchanges of Belmont through the agency of a letter symbolically come to life:

> Here is a letter, lady,
> The paper as the body of my friend,
> And every word in it a gaping wound
> Issuing life-blood, (III. ii. 263—6)

the distinction between Bassanio's fantasy of wealth and the actual nature of his wealth comes to the surface:

> Gentle lady,
> When I did first impart my love to you,
> I freely told you all the wealth I had
> Ran in my veins: I was a gentleman;
> And then I told you true. And yet, dear lady,
> Rating myself at nothing, you shall see
> How much I was a braggart: when I told you
> My state was nothing, I should then have told you
> That I was worse than nothing; for indeed
> I have engag'd myself to a dear friend,
> Engag'd my friend to his mere enemy,
> To feed my means. (III. ii. 252—63)

Although "to give and hazard all" when all he has runs in his veins may seem to be for Bassanio a form of mortal danger, only Antonio, who has distinctly material wealth, risks losing his blood (cf. "my bloody creditor", III. iii. 34, and "I'll pay it instantly with all my heart", IV. i. 281). When Bassanio hazards all for lead—and for Portia—he has nothing to lose, precisely because his wealth runs in his veins; if he loses his fortune, he will still remain who he is and "a gentleman". This is another version of wealth as a quality, as something innate, but here we see how the view of wealth as an innate quality must be "fed" by external wealth, acquired material possession.

Bassanio's borrowing from Antonio in order to make his hazard in Belmont does not lead to a mutual risk—Bassanio's blood, Antonio's gold; rather, only in bourgeois Venice do the protagonists experience or feel the consequences of Belmont hazardry: aristocratic credit, the "rich blood" that "speaks" for Bassanio in Belmont (III. ii. 176), completely depends on both the wealth and the blood of Antonio, the Merchant of Venice. Likewise, the Belmont environment, which allows for and enshrines indulgence, cannot be conceived of apart from its material superfluity; the fantasy that one should hazard all for love, that material things do not matter because true wealth lies within—"so may the outward shows be least themselves" (73)—requires faith in a strict correspondence between one's inner worth and an outward material abundance, supplied from elsewhere.

The antithetic second world keeps that "elsewhere" separated from the here and now. In the second world, the protagonists transform hazarding all into a sport, in order to free themselves from the consequences of the hazardry: the casket lottery, although it threatens loss, feels like a game, whereas the Venetian contracts, which threaten material loss, feel ominous and deadly serious. Further, the material abundance in the second world has no clear source or cause: the source of Bassanio's wealth would never have become an issue had not the Venetian messengers intruded on the Belmont rituals; Shakespeare pointedly leaves obscure the sources of Portia's family's wealth and of Antonio's restored fortune. But if one argues that *The Merchant of Venice* contains separate worlds of material and spiritual wealth, one has accepted the characters' voluntary illusions; the play once more dramatizes the "single nature's double name" proposition: the bourgeois material conditions that create the fluctuations of fortune in Venice guarantee—we might say "underwrite"—the stable abundance of Belmont and thereby enable the protagonists to abandon temporarily the responsibilities of the everyday world, enable them to assert that inner, spiritual qualities determine one's true worth.

"ABOVE THIS SCEPTRED SWAY" *The Trial*

The material interdependence of the primary and second worlds becomes especially apparent in *The Merchant of Venice* in part because the structure of the play allows Portia to reverse the locations of everyday and holiday, thus making it clear that retreat to the second world requires an attitude toward one's place rather than a removal to a specific place. In the other double-world comedies the protagonists make a single retreat. All of the protagonists move toward the wood outside Athens, the forest of Arden, Illyria; as they translate their societies from one location to another we become aware of the fundamental consistency of the system of class relations in each play. Although *The Merchant of Venice* begins in Venetian melancholy and ends with all the aristocratic protagonists celebrating the heavenly harmonies of Belmont, it contains within itself elements of a return passage to the everyday world of commercial affairs. Shakespeare designs the return to Venice—the trial, which interrupts the marriage rites of Bassanio and Portia, Gratiano and Nerissa—to emphasize the continuity between rather than the disjunction of the dramatic worlds: whereas when Bassanio journeys from Belmont back to Venice he returns to the material world of time and money, when Portia makes the same journey she does so as a retreat to a second world.

Portia begins her "retreat" to Venice by developing a paranoid fantasy; she performs a verbal act of dream-like economic compression in order to incorporate Shylock's attack on Antonio into her own soul. Antonio, she reasons, must be like Bassanio; Bassanio's soul resembles hers; therefore by attacking Antonio's body, Shylock also attacks Portia's soul:

> in companions
> That do converse and waste the time together,
> Whose souls do bear an egall yoke of love,
> There must be needs a like proportion
> Of lineaments, of manners, and of spirit;
> Which makes me think that this Antonio,
> Being the bosom lover of my lord,
> Must needs be like my lord. If it be so,

How little is the cost I have bestowed
In purchasing the semblance of my soul,
From out the state of hellish cruelty. (III. iv. 11–21)

Portia responds to her experience of cruelty by adopting masculine
disguise, and, like Rosalind in *As You Like It*, she does so initially as
a psychological rather than a dramatic strategy—the plot does not
require the disguise nor does the disguise advance the plot. Portia
isolates the playful and the sexual aspects of her disguise; her "work
in hand" (57) becomes a game as she talks to Nerissa only of the
fun they will have in playing at being men. She senses neither the
difficulty of their task nor the potential consequences of their
success or failure. Portia transforms the attempt to purchase the
semblance of her soul out of hellish cruelty into a joyous practical
joke and a playful competition between two women.

Portia's playful transformation contains, however, a distinct
aspect of homosexual aggression; she associates masculinity with
an aggressive control and dominance, the obvious counterpart to
her feelings of subjection ("so is the will of a living daughter curb'd
by the will of a dead father", I. ii. 24–5) and entrapment (her
picture and her future locked in the leaden casket) as a woman.
Consequently, Portia emphasizes the sexuality, and sometimes the
attendant violence, in the masculine roles that she and Nerissa will
adopt:

. . . they shall think we are accomplished
With what we lack; (III. iv. 61–62)

I'll prove the prettier fellow of the two,
And wear my dagger with the braver grace; (64–5)

. . . and tell quaint lies
How honorable ladies sought my love,
Which I denying, they fell sick and died.
I could not do withal. Then I'll repent,
And wish, for all that, that I had not kill'd them. (69–73)

Although Portia adopts some of the superficial feelings associated with retreat to the second world, she treats disaster as if it
were a game, her disguise allows her to engage in action rather than

to retreat from action. Once in Venice, Portia subdues the playfulness inherent in her disguise and acts so as to oppose directly Shylock's antagonism. Yet the nature of the direct action that Portia takes, the exact way in which she opposes Shylock's antagonism, makes us wonder: why must Portia create for herself such a central and dramatic role in Antonio's trial? The safest course would have been to commission Bellario to appear at the trial and state his venerable opinion regarding the law against an alien's seeking the life of "any citizen" (IV. i. 348 – 51); by ensuring her own participation in the trial, Portia jeopardizes Antonio and, indirectly, Bassanio. Although Portia may be hazarding all she has, she, like Bassanio, risks someone else's fortune to do so. But Portia's adoption of disguise, like Rosalind's retention of disguise in *As You Like It*, has no practical relation to the plot; Portia's disguise allows her to formulate her own impractical dramatic plot, and as such reveals her styles and attitudes, shows us how she sees herself in and presents herself to the world. And like all other manifestations of style in Shakespeare's works, Portia's dramatization (melodramatization?) of the trial scene expresses an ideology.

From the inside, from the point of view of the participants in the trial, Portia seems to construct a brilliant legal quibble, but from the outside, as the audience and Portia herself see her actions, Portia's playfulness becomes the predominant quality in the scene. Portia delays the outcome of the trial, and makes the outcome dependent on her presence, because she treats the trial as a game: from her point of view, Portia maintains throughout her stay in Venice the jocularity with which she departed Belmont. She carries with her the holiday spirit that Bassanio feels he has temporarily left behind. Just as Portia's money seems to fill out the economic scarcity of Venice, to replace and multiply the three thousand ducats that, as Heine first noted, Antonio, in spite of all of his merchant friends, could not raise,[6] Portia's holiday attitude, her immoderate, excessive, and superfluous passion (III. ii. 111 – 14), fills out the empty legalisms of the trial with passionate moral abundance. But in treating the trial as a game, as a forum for playing and acting, Portia intentionally disregards the consequences, for others, of her actions. In order to transform the trial into her game, Portia must place her own needs before the possibility that Antonio might be murdered. As a result, dis-

sociation and disjunction characterize the trial scene, for the scene
itself contains two distinct movements: the violent antagonism
between Antonio and Shylock reaches a climax when Portia
presents her legal quibble, and gets fully resolved when Shylock
departs defeated; Portia's serene playfulness accepts the defeat of
Shylock as an incident, and then proceeds independent of the
resolution of the crisis as Portia tries to get Bassanio's ring to play
out the next stage in her practical joke. Because the trial scene
depends on the simultaneity of an inside view as a critical case in
law and Portia's outside view as a development of a game or love-
plot, the scene uses a double sense of the significance of time. One
aspect of the trial scene, time-bound, or controlled by an imposed,
objective time, moves through periods of tension and crisis,
whereas the other aspect, created by Portia, like a holiday or
pastoral plot, develops by a series of unrelated incidents and derives
its sense of time from the subjective needs of the protagonists.

In the trial scene, the two time schemes characteristic of
Shakespeare's comedies intersect: Portia's holiday sense of the
subjective time that grows out of game and ritual proceeds
alongside of the Venetian everyday, objective time controlled by
debts, bonds, and contracts. Portia makes the events in the primary
world dependent on her actions; her game consists of controlling
the fate of others, while she keeps her own actions independent of
the fates she controls: her presence at the trial, like the second world
itself, offers to the protagonists a separate mode of value,
perception, and coherence. Her emphasis on mercy is a part of this,
in that she both incorporates mercy into natural processes and
places it above earthly termporality:

> It droppeth as the gentle rain from heaven
> Upon the place beneath; (IV. i. 185–6)

>   . . . it becomes
> The throned monarch better than his crown.
> His sceptre shows the force of temporal power,
> The attribute to awe and majesty,
> Wherein doth sit the dread and fear of kings;
> But mercy is above this sceptred sway,
> It is enthroned in the hearts of kings,
> It is an attribute to God himself. (188–95)

The mercy that Portia proposes would elevate human actions "above this sceptred sway" of time and of earthly power, and thereby would consciously transcend the strictures of objective time and of retributive justice, associated with "penalty and forfeit", (207), with money, repayment, and measurement.

The particular version of mercy that Portia proposes, analogous with the holiday morality of the second world, reformulates the class contents of the comedy. The charge that one "must" forgive one's debtors develops as a challenge to the bourgeois economy from within the aristocratic fantasy of superfluous and organic wealth, wealth in the veins. Portia's moral imperatives differ from those within the Venetian economic system: the Venetians regret that the Duke "cannot deny the course of law", (III. iii. 26; cf., III. ii. 277—79, IV. i. 101—2) although they "all expect a gentle answer" (34) from Shylock; Portia sees mercy itself as an imperative that negates the "course of justice", (199). These two opposed sets of imperatives derive from the opposed economic conditions of scarcity and surfeit; the course of justice regulates and determines legal possession of material goods, of property rights, whereas the quality of mercy represents an attitude toward distribution, which purports to be concerned with moral behavior independent of material possession.

The Venetians must maintain mercy as a separate ideal; were it incorporated into their society it would obliterate the economic foundations upon which all of their institutions depend. The Venetians embody and enact a double attitude toward mercy: they can be vengeful, retributive, and threatening toward the alien Shylock—"The Jew shall have all justice" (321)—while maintaining that they "render him" mercy, particularly by offering him the opportunity to become a Christian (378, 386—7). That is, the bourgeois Christian community produces *both* the vicious sarcasm of Gratiano and the ethical idealism of Portia; the extremes do not exclude, nor do they balance, each other: they are extremes that accompany a unified moral and dramatic process. The Jew-baiting extends, in the realm of morals, the economic "hold" that the laws of Venice have only on aliens (347—51): Gratiano gives direct verbal expression to the moral principles implicit in the legal structure of Venice. At the same time, Portia expresses the fantasy that the extant system of legal economic relations extends beyond concern for material possession and derives its validity from natural and heavenly sanction.

Mercy functions in Venetian society not as an active moral principle but as an expressed ideal: mercy works as the bourgeois version of the aristocratic, second-world moral system of hazarding all. Portia argues that in order to receive mercy, we first must "render /The deeds of mercy", (201−2) just as in Belmont absolute risk must precede absolute gain. But because of the organic, intrinsic nature of aristocratic wealth, the Belmont morality contains no risk of material loss: hazarding all becomes significant as a gesture precisely because it is isolated from potential consequences. Because the Venetians, however, treat all wealth as inorganic, barren, strictly material (and therefore, they argue, wealth should not accumulate interest, or breed, I. iii. 94−6, 134−5), the principles of mercy, if applied in Venice as a moral sanction, would necessitate actual material sacrifice. As a result, mercy, like hazarding all in Belmont, becomes a detached concept, separated from the financial operations that constitute the social life of Venice.

As an ideal isolated from the economic forces of Venice, mercy superimposes a system of absolute wealth upon the limited and unstable economic resources of Venice. By introducing mercy, Portia turns the bourgeois moral system upside down; Portia isolates Shylock from the rest of bourgeois society, making him in fact an alien, and allows the other Venetians to transform their material dependence into its opposite, moral superiority to wealth. Mercy enables the bourgeoisie to become aristocratic.

Ordinarily, the bourgeois morality of Venice, the dependence on material acquisition, would be incompatible with the idealist system of the second world, the faith that wealth, by its nature, correlates with one's fixed class status. During the trial, mercy becomes a gesture toward such a system, and as such draws the bourgeoisie and the Belmont aristocracy together within one unified attitude. The bourgeois society can believe that its acquisitive actions, the legal seizure of Shylock's property, in effect show mercy and hence distributive generosity; further, the bourgeoisie can believe that the Venetian legal and economic institutions are earthly manifestations of a higher, more perfect order of things. The trial scene introduces Christian morality into *The Merchant of Venice* so as to allow the bourgeoisie access to aristocratic fantasies of independence from material conditions and of participation in the heavenly system of natural harmony.

IRONY

The protagonists do not live up to the standards that they themselves establish and avow. They are, in a word, hypocritical. This does not, however, make *The Merchant of Venice* an ironic comedy, a play meant to expose or to "place" the moral shortcomings and limitations of the protagonists. Such a reading effectively responds to the romantic and allegorical interpretations, which have attempted to explain away all of the quite blatant hypocrisy and cruelty in the Christian community, but the ironic reading creates its own distortion of the drama. An ironic reading depends on the assumption that one can separate the form from the contents of the drama: in *The Merchant of Venice* the irony would result from the protagonists' being unworthy of the harmonic resolution which the comic form brings them toward. In this sense the protagonists would be "placed", in that there would develop a distance or a gap between the harmonic conclusion of the comic form and the dissonant contents of the actions throughout the drama. The gap between these two imagined places would measure the dramatic irony.[7]

It is difficult to see what this gap would signify. Shakespeare allows no directly ironic contents to intervene in the formal conclusion, and he thereby insulates the play from the explicitly satirical qualities of *Troilus and Cressida*, or the implicit ones of *Measure for Measure*. If Shakespeare meant the play to be ironic, I do not see why he would rely on an irony of absence, or an irony located solely in the audience without any dramatic characters who can participate in the audience response. The ironic reading, it seems, misunderstands the relation between form and contents in Shakespeare's comedies; the contents do not fill out the predetermined form, either completely or leaving ironic gaps, but, to paraphrase Fredric Jameson, the form extends the deeper logic of the contents.[8] The dramatic contents create the particular dramatic form of *The Merchant of Venice*; the joyous conclusion does not indicate a separation between the protagonists' ideals and their behavior, but expresses an ideal logically developed from the dramatic action.

This makes sense only in so far as we understand the ideals of Belmont as the ideals of a specific social class, and as the created solution to opposition between social classes. The meditation on universal harmony and on the relativity of ethics and aesthetics, the enforced and deliberate tendency toward play, demonstrate the aristocratic ability, derived from faith in a fixed social structure and in an unending supply of wealth, to transcend bourgeois threats and oppositions. The Belmont ideals constitute a strategic response to the Venetian insistence that wealth can be purchased by the weight and thus that time, money, and value are external and objective qualities. The aristocracy responds to this bourgeois ideology by reorganizing the attitude toward time, from Antonio's belief that time is spent (I. i. 153) to Portia's that time is wasted (III. iv. 12):[9] the aristocracy transforms life from work to game and ritual. This subjective aristocratic perception, through the course of the drama, finds objective statement and existence as a world—Belmont, the second world, the world of holiday—and thereby gets incorporated into nature, receives material status. The aristocratic second world acquires an objective presence, but its objectivity is meaningful only within the larger context of the dialectical opposition between classes and as an antithetic term opposed to the bourgeois primary world, Venice.

The Merchant of Venice dramatizes the same dialectical process through which class relationships and antagonisms develop in history: the dramatic contents turn into their opposite as they are objectified into dramatic form, as they become the second world and the harmonic conclusion. Just as contents become form, the subjective feelings of the ruling class become objective, part of the hierarchic system of nature. *The Merchant of Venice* dramatizes process and transformation; whenever the play becomes fixed in one attitude, it does so in order to characterize the leisurely, aristocratic sense of time as a subjective quality: the poetic meditations of Salerio and Salanio on Antonio's fortune, of Bassanio on Portia's portrait, and especially of Jessica and Lorenzo on the heavens and on music delineate the aristocratic mind and distinguish it from the bourgeois mind. Whereas the aristocrats meditate at leisure, for the bourgeoisie every word counts: as Mark Van Doren has observed, Shylock "is always repeating phrases,

half to himself, as misers do—hoarding them if they are good".[10]
Irony would negate the process and transformation, and would fix
the entire drama in one place: the ironic reading gives the comic
ideals their own objectivity, not an objectivity created from within
and by a social class, and the ironic reading measures a distance
between the placed protagonists and the predetermined moral
ideals. The ironic reading criticizes the aristocratic protagonists for
not living up to their ideals, but it does not criticize the aristocratic
ideals as such, for it fails to see that the ideals emerge from and
express the needs of a particular social class.

Irony is, therefore, itself a second-world strategy, in that it
attempts to fix a dialectical process in one objective moment in
time and in one arrangement in space: irony tends, very much like
the aristocratic language in *The Merchant of Venice* and elsewhere
in Shakespeare's works, to arrest time through rhetorical contemplation of an object, emotion, or condition. As such, the ironic
reading of *The Merchant of Venice*, although it may seem to derive
from historical principles in that it criticizes the aristocratic
hypocrisy, fundamentally opposes dialectical analysis: it treats the
social classes in isolation, it ignores the aristocratic origin of the
comic form, and it treats actions and ideals as fixed, separate
conditions instead of as created antitheses within a single dialectical
process.

3 *A Midsummer Night's Dream*

"SUCH SEPARATION AS MAY WELL BE SAID"
The Athenian Lovers

In *A Midsummer Night's Dream* the romantic protagonists, confronted with obstacles, retreat from the primary world. Two of the Athenian lovers, Hermia and Lysander, find themselves confronted by, and they willfully oppose, three distinct kinds of obstacles: the law, the state, and the family. Hermia and Lysander wish to marry against the will of Hermia's father Egeus, against the advice of Duke Theseus, and in defiance of the abstract "law of Athens", which, theoretically, transcends human desire, will, and judgment, which, Theseus says, "by no means we may extenuate" (I. i. 119—20). The two lovers do not try to outwit or to deceive Hermia's father, to circumvent the law of Athens, or to win each other through violence, vengeance, or heroics. They oppose these obstacles by devising a strategy of replacement, escape to somewhere beyond the reach of "the sharp Athenian law" (162); they hope to find in a new location the liberating alternative to the restrictions of Athenian civilization. The law of Athens deprives Hermia and Lysander of independence and autonomy; it considers Hermia no more than an object, a piece of property to be disposed of by Egeus:

> I beg the ancient privilege of Athens:
> As she is mine, I may dispose of her;
> Which shall be either to this gentleman,
> Or to her death, according to our law
> Immediately provided in that case; (I. i. 41—5)

or, what may be worse, molded by him:

37

> To you your father should be as a god;
> One that compos'd your beauties; yea, and one
> To whom you are but as a form in wax,
> By him imprinted, and within his power,
> To leave the figure, or disfigure it. (I. i. 47–51)

Confronted by Egeus' will, neither Hermia's choice nor Lysander's qualities matter, for the law of Athens subordinates human qualities and subjective judgments to the abstract systems of hierarchy and possession within both family and state:

> For you, fair Hermia, look you arm yourself
> To fit your fancies to your father's will;
> Or else the law of Athens yields you up . . . . (I. i. 117–9)

By escaping to the forest, the romantic protagonists attempt to replace an abstract, objective system with subjective, personal judgments, a "father's voice" (54) with their own eyes.

But the play does not sustain these easy distinctions between youth and age, subjective and objective, liberation and restriction: these distinctions initiate the play but do not dominate it. The Athenian forest never becomes a second world, a version of pastoral. The initial association of the Athenian legal system with oppression and tyranny dissolves, and oppression reassembles *within* the forest, in a different, more personal, form. In the forest, subjective, internal oppositions replace and intensify the external obstacles that the protagonists had hoped to escape. Once Hermia and Lysander escape Athens and become ostensibly free to choose love with their own eyes, the vicissitudes of their subjective judgments become obstacles to romantic resolution; it is as if freedom to choose makes choice impossible. Once the lovers enter the forest, the supposed autonomy of love's judgments becomes reduced to pure mechanism; the play assigns the subjective judgments that the lovers think to be their own to an external source, the magic potion. Their own wills, that is, materialize as a specific external obstacle. By attributing the subjective judgments to an objectified, outside source, Shakespeare demonstrates a structural continuity between the forest and the court: without the fairy magic, the play would break down into worlds of objective and subjective oppression; the inclusion of an easily identifiable objective motive for the protagonists' supposedly subjective choices demonstrates that any supposedly private, subjective action (the choice of true love, for example) has objective, social contents, which escape from the codified, objective laws of everyday society does not negate. The forest allows the protagonists to escape the father's will and the law of Athens, but, as the magic potion indicates, an external authority controls the seemingly subjective choices that the lovers make in the forest—and afterwards.

This ambiguous quality of the forest in *A Midsummer Night's Dream*—as both alternative and repetition—does not appear when Lysander first proposes the escape from Athens. Lysander suggests that he and Hermia escape to the house of his "widow aunt, a dowager, /Of great revenue", (I. i. 157–8). Duke Theseus has already had his say about dowagers: in a gratuitous comparison, he has declared that the slowly waning old moon (he will not marry until "four happy days bring in /Another moon"; 2–3) "lingers my desire, /Like to a step-dame, or a dowager, /Long withering out a young man's revenue" (I. i. 4–6). Shakespeare uses the word *dowager* twice in this scene; it occurs in none of his previous works, and it occurs in no other work on which he did not collaborate. But here the recurrence, with opposite connotations, of this unusual word indicates the extent to which Lysander and Theseus have opposite perceptions. The same force that metaphorically prevents Theseus's fulfillment and that deprives him of revenue to which he feels entitled appears to Lysander as a force that incorporates him into a financial, familial, and sexual community: "And she respects me as her only son. /There, gentle Hermia, may I marry thee" (160–1). The perceptual opposition between the two men, using *dowager* as a verbal bridge, crosses into a political opposition: Lysander proposes a liberating world, discontinuous with the laws of Theseus's dukedom; in Lysander's world one's social and familial superiors would accumulate wealth in order to bestow it, and elders would sanction rather than oppose his subjective decisions. In short, Lysander envisions a second world in which he and Hermia will be accepted by a benevolent, nurturing society.

Lysander's initial vision of the second-world alternative colors and tends to distort our perception of what he and Hermia actually accomplish by and during their retreat. Their attempt to escape to the dowager's, as we learn when we first see them in the forest, fails; Hermia is "faint with wand'ring in the wood" because Lysander has "forgot" their "way" (II. ii. 35—6). Shakespeare, in fact, confines their retreat to the forest, and keeps the forest within the reach of the Athenian social system. Hermia and Lysander escape to the same place where the fairies have gathered, "come from the farthest steep of India," (II. i. 69) to celebrate Theseus's wedding, the same place where the craftsmen have met to prepare for their participation in the Duke's wedding ceremony. The escape from Athenian law has led the lovers to the single place in the whole world most intensely concentrated on the confirmation and celebration of Athenian hierarchy and social custom; the forest to which the protagonists have retreated is dominated by the Athenian laws of degree and possession—the "palace wood", "the Duke's oak" (I. ii. 101, 110).

While trying to get beyond one set of laws, the formal Athenian laws, the lovers—both couples—stay within the confines of social laws, the laws of decorum and propriety. Lysander's rival, Demetrius, suggests that now that he is outside the city, he is not bound by its laws, and that he therefore may rape the woman who pursues him, Helena:

> You do impeach your modesty too much,
> To leave the city and commit yourself
> Into the hands of one that loves you not;
> To trust the opportunity of night,
> And the ill counsel of a desert place,
> With the rich worth of your virginity. (II. i. 214—9)

Helena replies, undaunted:

> Your virtue is my privilege. (220)

This is a telling exchange: Helena presumes that even beyond the codified legal system of the city an internalized code will govern and restrict Demetrius's behavior; beneath her surface assumption runs the current of her own need. Despite her pursuit of Demetrius, she requires some kind of protection against physical ravishment, against violation of her internalized moral code.

Hermia and Lysander also have transported to the forest the

system of Athenian moral conventions, and it is nearly their undoing. As they lie down to go to sleep in the forest, Hermia implores Lysander:

> But, gentle friend, for love and courtesy,
> Lie further off, in humane modesty;
> Such separation as may well be said
> Becomes a virtuous bachelor and a maid,
> So far be distant. . . . (II. ii. 56–60)

Lysander acquiesces. Moments later, Puck enters and misreads the empty space between the two lovers:

> Pretty soul, she durst not lie
> Near this lack-love, this kill-courtesy. (76–7)

That is, the forest spirit can interpret the "separation" only as one of antipathy; he has no sense of the transported city-manners that derive from an abstract moral and social convention that requires a physical separation between two lovers. Puck's failure to comprehend how real moral abstractions can be to the young Athenians, how the abstraction of social convention and the fear of moral censure can govern their sensual lives and experiences, almost destroys the romantic bond between the two.

The separation between the virtuous bachelor and the maid can be taken as a dramatic representation—an emblem—of the Athenian social code, which separates people from each other and from their senses and emotions. The separation correlates with the Athenian law and the father's will, both of which try to dictate and enforce the romantic responses of others, to replace subjective perception with external and imposed authority. The lovers flee Athens so as to win autonomy, but their actions remain systematic and codified, based on received ideas rather than on their own judgments, visions, or senses.[1] The strictest possible conventionality circumscribes the escape to the forest in *A Midsummer Night's Dream*, and thereby protects the forest, or the lovers in the forest, from sensuality. The lovers continually use language, especially the language of pastoral and romantic convention, to protect themselves from sexual and violent physical encounters, and, by doing so, they substitute an external system for their own perceptions.

While in the forest they reiterate, in a different form, the authoritarian social system that controls Athenian love.

In a sense, then, language and literary references function so as to re-create, in the forest, the prohibitions expressed, at court, by the laws of Athens: language keeps the lovers apart. This authoritarian and restrictive function of language helps define the role of the imagination in *A Midsummer Night's Dream*. As R. W. Dent has argued, *A Midsummer Night's Dream*, again and again, seems to draw our attention to "the role of imagination in love and in art", (p. 115) and to its own status as "the product of Shakespeare's own imagination" (p. 122); it does not follow, however, that the play offers us a "disarmingly unpretentious defense of poetry" (p. 129).[2] Rather, as I shall try to demonstrate, the play shows us the *use* of the imagination, the function of the imagination in society: throughout *A Midsummer Night's Dream* the imagination has both a creative and a discriminatory function. In *A Midsummer Night's Dream* the imagination, by enforcing separation, asserts and creates a distance between the self and the other, and thereby it protects the self and creates an implicit hierarchy: the separation between the self and the other has an ideological as well as a protective and conventional function. Initially, the lovers use the imagination to deny the sensual reality of one another and thereby to incorporate the Athenian prohibitions into their own judgments; later, when the entire act of retreat has been reincorporated into Athenian aristocratic society, the aristocracy itself uses the imagination to establish an hierarchical separation between itself and the other social classes that constitute Athenian society. In fact, the imagination, and not the forest, functions in *A Midsummer Night's Dream* as the second world: it expresses particular interests, initially personal and later class, as if they were universal interests and it protects those interests against the interests of others.

Language, as it isolates the lovers from one another and perverts their rebellious actions, works to keep the Athenian laws and conventions intact. From the outset, language forces Hermia and Lysander to work against their own best interests and thereby to keep their escape within the reach of Athenian convention: they "unfold" their "minds" to Helena, giving their private compact a public status, making it a story, and immeasurably increasing the likelihood of their being intercepted. Helena repeats and thereby emphasizes this tendency to use language so as to ensure the failure

of one's actions when she departs vowing to tell Demetrius of
Hermia's plan:

> Then to the wood will he to-morrow night
> Pursue her; and for this intelligence
> If I have thanks, it is a dear expense. (I. i. 247—9)

Helena quite obviously acts against her own best interests, in so far
as her interests are identical with winning Demetrius; her real
interests, however, may be more complex, may not all be
conscious. In the same action with which she willfully imposes an
obstacle between herself and Demetrius, she also restores the verbal
contents of her love for Demetrius. For Helena, "love looks not
with the eyes but with the mind", (234) and consequently she
laments the loss of a verbal rather than a physical Demetrius;
whereas Hermia, she thinks, has a physical relationship ("heat",
"melt") to Demetrius, Helena remembers her own relationship to
Demetrius in terms of language, of "oaths":

> For ere Demetrius look'd on Hermia's eyne,
> He hail'd down oaths that he was only mine;
> And when this hail some heat from Hermia felt,
> So he dissolv'd, and show'rs of oaths did melt. (I. i. 242—5)

In going to "tell him of fair Hermia's flight", (246) Helena restores
the verbal or the narrative aspect of her dissolved love affair with
Demetrius: she replaces the lost physical love with words.

Likewise, Hermia and Lysander experience love as a literary
process; when they talk of love they talk not of each other but of
what they have read. Lysander's lamentation, which introduces the
plan to escape from Athens, derives from his consciousness not of
love, but of narratives about love:

> Ay me! for aught that I could ever read,
> Could ever hear by tale or history,
> The course of true love never did run smooth . . .
>
> (I. i. 132—4)

The lovers are so aware of language that they have no awareness of
one another. Hermia and Lysander spend most of the first scene

talking at cross-purposes: Lysander inverts Hermia's stoical argument ("Then let us teach our trial patience", 152) into an invi-
tation to run away ("A good persuasion; therefore hear me,
Hermia . . . Steal forth thy father's house to-morrow night", 156;
164): Lysander takes Hermia's assurance "by all the vows that ever
men have broke" (175) as a "promise" (179). Language freezes
into the formulas of literary convention and thereby turns into an
object; once this process begins, once the characters use language as
a thing instead of as a medium, language becomes a barrier
between the lovers rather than a means of communication.

The isolation imposed by language becomes more rigid and
more obvious once the lovers reach the forest; there, acts of the
imagination, absorption in literary style, become so predominant
that the characters perceive one another as verbal beings, re-
positories of literary convention. When Lysander wakes up,
charmed into loving Helena, he looks at her eyes and sees not
physical beauty, but literature:

> Reason becomes the marshal to my will,
> And leads me to your eyes, where I o'erlook
> Love's stories written in Love's richest book. (II. ii. 120—2)

Demetrius awakens into a set of Petrarchan and pseudo-classical
conventions:

> O Helen, goddess, nymph, perfect, divine!
> To what, my love, shall I compare thine eyne?
> Crystal is muddy. O, how ripe in show
> Thy lips, those kissing cherries, tempting grow!
> That pure congealed white, high Taurus' snow,
> Fann'd with the eastern wind, turns to a crow
> When thou hold'st up thy hand. (III. ii. 137—43)

Hermia, similarly, perceives Lysander as only a collection of
words. She makes Lysander's "lying" pun ("Then by your side no
bed-room me deny; /For lying so, Hermia, I do not lie", II. ii. 51—
2) into a real crux. By making him "lie further off", Hermia forces
Lysander to adopt the alternative sense of "lying"; in forcing him
to adopt the rhetorical rather than the physical sense of the verb to
lie, she reduces his lanugage to verbal mechanism, to pretty

riddling. It follows that Hermia first notes Lysander's desertion as a verbal absence:

> What, out of hearing gone? No sound, no word?
> Alack, where are you? Speak, and if you hear . . .
> (II. ii. 152−3)

and that she finds him again by pursuing his language:

> Thou are not by mine eye, Lysander, found;
> Mine ear, I thank it, brought me to thy sound.
> (III. ii. 181−2)

Helena interprets the adoration suddenly offered her as nothing but words, and therefore as nothing:

> These vows are Hermia's. Will you give her o'er?
> Weigh oath with oath, and you will nothing weigh.
> Your vows to her and me, put in two scales,
> Will even weigh; and both as light as tales. (III. ii. 130−3)

She correctly notices the one-sidedly linguistic, and conventional, quality of the male lovers' behavior—"to vow, and swear, and superpraise my parts, /When I am sure you hate me with your hearts" (153−4). But her childishly paranoid fantasy misinterprets the offered affection as nothing but a conventional arrangement of words, an act:

> Ay, do! persever, counterfeit sad looks,
> Make mouths upon me when I turn my back,
> Wink each at other, hold the sweet jest up;
> This sport, well carried, shall be chronicled. (III. ii. 237−40)

She uses *her* imagination to turn Demetrius and Lysander into actors, and thereby to purge their actions of sexual impulses. Since she sees the advances only as acts or as material for composition, she can become an appreciative audience—

> Lysander: My love, my life, my soul, fair Helena!
> Helena: O excellent! (246−7)

—as opposed to a physical participant in the action.

Hermia assumes that the hatred that she experiences derives directly from a rhetorical act:

> "Puppet"? Why so? Ay, that way goes the game.
> Now I perceive that she hath made compare
> Between our statures: she hath urg'd her height. . . .
>
> (III. ii. 289—91)

It is not so much Helena's height, Hermia believes, as the rhetorical tactic with which she "urged" her height that has won Lysander. Hermia consequently isolates and focuses on, and projects an aggressive quality onto, each of Helena's words of diminuation:

> "Little" again? Nothing but "low" and "little"?
> Why will you suffer her to flout me thus? (326—7)

But precisely because Helena flouts Hermia *thus*—with words— Hermia is protected from physical combat. Words have replaced bodies.

Language continually intervenes within the couples, or the couplings; just as language replaces sex between lovers, so language replaces violence between rivals. Lysander's rivalry, from the first, is with the word *Demetrius*:

> Where is Demetrius? O, how fit a word
> Is that vile name to perish on my sword! (II. ii. 106—7)

Language ensures that Lysander and Demetrius fight without physical violence; in their linguistic frenzy the opposition between speech and action conveniently dissolves. Speech seems to stimulate violent action:

> Lysander: I swear by that which I will lose for thee,
>   To prove him false that says I love thee not.
> Demetrius: I say I love thee more than he can do.
> Lysander: If thou say so, withdraw, and prove it too.
>
> (III. ii. 252—5)

When they go off "cheek by jowl" to fight each other, however, language obstructs or protects them, separates them, because they follow Puck's words rather than each other's bodies.

With his disembodied voice, Puck keeps the rivals physically separated. Yet his verbal intervention constitutes more than a mechanical and comic plot device for breaking up the fight. Throughout the play, language, especially conventional literary formulation, protects each of the lovers from physical violence and from sexual aggression. When the verbal intervention fails as protection, when the lovers *think* they have come nearest to assaulting one another, the lovers in fact have directed their violence toward language itself, or toward a figuration of disembodied language: they run through the woods in pursuit of Puck's words. Their attack on language succeeds in every way: the night in the forest ends with each of the four lovers safe, separate, and in silence.

"I WILL OVERBEAR YOUR WILL" *Theseus*

The lovers wake up in very unusual circumstances. The leading figure of primary-world authority hovers over them, asking them to explain their actions, to explain the "concord" ostensibly achieved during their absence from Athens. But the authority figure does not appear harsh and recriminating; he has relinquished his strict adherence to, or administration of, the abstract structure of authority, the laws of the state. Because the lovers have externalized or purged their fears and hatreds during the verbal chaos and literary excesses of the night in the forest, they seem to have achieved a new harmony, a "gentle concord", not just as couples but among one another and within each one's psyche. This achieved concord has, apparently, a sympathetic effect, "in the world" (IV. i. 143): the will of the Duke reverses so as to certify, rather than to obstruct, the romantic resolutions that the young protagonists have achieved and had thrust upon them. Authority joins with youth to reject the irrational will of the old man:

> Fair lovers, you are fortunately met;
> Of this discourse we more will hear anon.
> Egeus I will overbear your will;
> For in the temple, by and by, with us
> These couples shall eternally be knit. (IV. i. 177–81)

Confronted with this unusually optimistic modification of the Plautine comic model, we might ask of Shakespeare, with Theseus, "how comes this gentle concord in the world?" To understand the process of this resolution, we must place the romance aspect of *A Midsummer Night's Dream* within the wider social and imaginative context through which it develops. The flight to the forest, which when isolated as a pattern or a structure seems to be a direct challenge of or opposition to authority, to the autonomy of the state, remains very close, metaphorically and dramatically, to the paramount ruling-class consciousness in the play, the Duke's. In this sense, the pattern of rebellion against established order, fundamental to the Plautine model, has here been turned into its opposite; youth runs away so as to confirm or reaffirm the stability of the social order. It is important to realize that the flight to the forest, in some ways, satisfies Duke Theseus's needs and helps solidify his position as a figure of social authority.

The conjunction between the flight to the forest and Duke Theseus's consciousness appears in the first few passages in the play. Anticipating his marriage four days hence to Hippolyta, Theseus commands his master of the revels, Philostrate, to:

> Stir up Athenian youth to merriments,
> Awake the pert and nimble spirit of mirth,
> Turn melancholy forth to funerals:
> The pale companion is not for our pomp. (I. i. 12–15)

Philostrate exits, not having said a word; four lines later, enough time to allow for a very quick doubling of parts, Egeus enters, with Hermia, Lysander, and Demetrius in tow, to present his "complaint" to the Duke. The entire pastoral romance that Egeus' entry introduces responds, in a sense, to Theseus's call for merriment and enacts an intrinsic dramatic function subordinate to the Duke's call for pomp, triumph, and revelling (19). We can intensify and confirm this sense if we compare Act V with Act I: in Act V Theseus reiterates the call for revelry and entertainment to fill up the time before the consummation of his marriage:

> Come now; what masques, what dances shall we have,
> To wear away this long age of three hours
> Between [our] after-supper and bed-time?

Where is our usual manager of mirth?
What revels are in hand? Is there no play
To ease the anguish of a torturing hour?
Call Philostrate. (V. i. 32—8)

Theseus's psychological need and his strategic response to that need are repeated almost precisely: throughout the play Theseus uses art, acts of the imagination, to secure his own autonomy. His call for entertainment reduces the episode of the four lovers to the dramatic status of an interlude, an entertainment. In so far as the lovers have autonomy, this reduction cannot quite be justified, but Theseus's strategy partially aims to reduce and to incorporate what autonomy the lovers do have. From Theseus's point of view—the point of view that the play enforces—the pastoral retreat, like the masque of "Pyramus and Thisbe", emphasizes and secures the social status of the Athenian ruling class. The entire retreat to the forest, framed by Theseus's call for entertainment and his magnanimous transcendence of the law, functions in the first part of the play, as "Pyramus and Thisbe" will in the second, as an aesthetic act.

Neither aesthetic act, however, exists in isolation; rather, both fulfill important functions in Duke Theseus's civic strategy, his administration of the state. Theseus declares explicitly that his wedding celebration will use aesthetics, another "key", to gloss over the violent and destructive aspects of his history:

Hippolyta, I woo'd thee with my sword,
And won thy love doing thee injuries;
But I will wed thee in another key,
With pomp, with triumph, and with revelling. (I. i. 16—19)

The wedding and its attendant celebrations will constitute a complete substitution, replacement of physical violence with aesthetic forms and with the organized rituals and institutions of civilized behaviour. Theseus shows the same attitude of mind in the famous scene during which he describes his hounds to Hippolyta. Theseus shows more concern for aesthetic qualities—appearance and, especially, tone—and for breeding lines than for the hunting ability, the capacity to inflict injury; the hounds are "slow in pursuit; but match'd in mouth like bells, /Each under each",

(IV. i. 123—4). Theseus, it seems, has a heightened aesthetic sensibility, but Theseus's keen awareness of the power of beauty always has elements of what Howard Nemerov calls the "administrative" attitude toward art (636).[3] Theseus's aesthetics always appears as a conventional replacement of destructive human impulses, and as such forms a strategy by which he can replace disquietude with civil harmony. He facilitates the interrupted Plautine comedy as another of his opportunities to replace injury with civilization.

Theseus's sense of beauty restates that of the four lovers, but in a broader context. The lovers use literary convention to contain their own private sexual and violent drives, to replace consciousness of another's body with an exaggerated consciousness of language. Theseus applies this strategy to society at large: he both incorporates and objectifies the process of aristocratic rebellion enacted by the lovers in that he translates the political process of rebellion against his authority into an aesthetic act, a revel. In doing so Theseus takes the potential divisions that threaten the civil peace of his society and the autonomy of his class and makes division an aspect of a larger harmony and consistency. This at once reduces the challenge to Athenian law to an act of style and gesture, an aesthetic distraction, while it also subsumes the challenge within a process that ultimately negates the need for rebellion. We could almost say, with C. L. Barber, that the rebellion against the law momentarily releases and ultimately clarifies the law, but, as usual, Barber's formulation, ignoring the class contents of the rebellion, the way in which the rebellion serves the needs of only the ruling class, misses the social context for the resolution.[4] Because the escape from Athens remains consistently within the aesthetic limitations imposed by Duke Theseus, the final clarification renews the autonomy of the Duke and confirms the "natural" status of the Athenian social structure. The rebellion against the law, that is, stays separate from rebellion against the Duke, so that, once the law is clarified, the Duke can absorb back into the social system, without moral compromise and without relinquishing his autonomy, those aristocrats whose actions rebelled against the law. An autonomous figure of authority comprehends the turbulence, unrestraint, and whimsicality of the release/clarification movement in *A Midsummer Night's Dream*. It is therefore misleading and selective to say that *A Midsummer*

Night's Dream releases society from the traditional structure of
authority and degree; in fact, authority itself releases and then
reabsorbs the aristocratic protagonists so as to incorporate both
sides of the holiday/everyday opposition into its administration of
the state.

   Although I have spoken rather abstractly about "authority", in
A Midsummer Night's Dream authority seems almost indistinguish-
able from Duke Theseus: he is its agent, he bodies forth the abstract
concept. In this sense, he differs from his counterpart in *The
Merchant of Venice*, the Duke of Venice, who remains subordinate
to the abstract force of authority as codified and bodied forth in the
laws of the state. Theseus never rests in this position of subordination: initially he established himself as a mere administrator
of the law, but when he concludes the imaginative interlude and
reabsorbs the aristocratic rebellion into his own consciousness—
"with us/These couples shall eternally be knit"—he also subordinates the law to his subjective will, to his autonomy. The
establishment of civilized order in Athens depends on the
incorporation of authority into the subjective will of a single
individual: Theseus withdraws the sentence, but the law itself does
not change. Concord occurs when the figure of authority replaces
the objective restrictions of the civil code with the benevolence of
his own subjective will. The imaginative interlude in the forest
concludes by identifying the feeling of concord and liberation with
a complete dependence on Duke Theseus's autonomy.

"TO TAKE WHAT THEY MISTAKE" *Craftsmen and Fairies*

We expect a pastoral romance to allow a protagonist or group of
protagonists to reject the codified laws and traditions of the state,
the primary world, in order to discover a simpler life led in
accordance with the laws of nature. Ordinarily, the pastoral
protagonist will have a heightened awareness of the natural
environment that comprises the second world. This awareness can
take different forms: in *As You Like It*, for example, Duke Senior
speaks of both the advantages and hardships of life in Arden. In all
pastorals, however, nature replaces rigid, objective authority and
allows the protagonists to impose their own subjective wills on an
environment that appears to be both simple and, occasionally, in

harmony with some mysterious cosmic principle of benevolence: nature allows the protagonists to fulfill and to express their own natures. Outside of the consciousness of the aristocratic protagonists in the pastoral, however, nature, the second-world environment, seems to have its own autonomy and its own objective laws: for Corin, for example, the shepherd's life constitutes a form of everyday work, rather than an empty form to be filled with the contents of his fantasies.

In *A Midsummer Night's Dream*, nature, the conditions of the forest, neither passively reflects the needs of the protagonists nor autonomously imposes its own everyday aspect on their wills. Because the retreat to nature initiated by the romantic protagonists dissolves into the will of the primary-world authority figure, the state of nature in the forest never permits true independence from the forces of authority. Pastoral romance uses retreat to explore, from within the aristocratic consciousness, the relation between subjective will and nature, but in *A Midsummer Night's Dream* the pastoral retreat explores the relation between authority—not autonomy—and nature. Nature, in a sense, has become an active creation of the mind of the primary-world authority figure, Duke Theseus, and the romantic protagonists assume the role of passive recipients of the action: they let nature act upon and express itself through them.

While nature acts upon them, the protagonists in *A Midsummer Night's Dream* remain unaware of nature: just as language intervenes to protect them from consciousness of one another's bodies and to prevent physical violence, the excessive attention to style inhibits the lovers' sensory awareness of their environment. They show such attention to the nuances of one another's words and of the alterations in their own feelings that they never emerge from the closed circuit of pursuit, rejection, and jealousy that they establish in Athens and transport to the forest. Moreover, other components of the traditional pastoral vision present in the forest never take on the traditional pastoral associations in that they do not engage with the second-world aristocratic consciousness in any reciprocal way. Retreat to a second-world depends on and requires both the autonomy of one class, or group of characters, and the subordination of another class: the aristocratic leisure derives from others' labour. Within the forest itself, *A Midsummer Night's Dream* contains in rudimentary form both the autonomous and the subordinate groups: the fairies, as Barber has remarked, function very much like pastoral shepherds although without the labour of tending flock; the craftsmen function as a coarsened version of a class of servants, although they have no direct association with the aristocrats when within the forest. Both of these quasi-pastoral groups, however, retain explicit ties to the authoritarian structure that, according to the traditional pastoral form or formula, the protagonists would reject by retreating to the forest. In *A Midsummer Night's Dream* the craftsmen and the fairies, like the protagonists themselves, function as further extension and development of the primary-world, authoritarian consciousness. The pastoral components never cohere into a single autonomous pastoral structure that could work as an antithesis to the primary world. The comprehensiveness of the primary world, the ability of the laws, codes, and authority figures in Athens, to control and determine the romantic protagonists' subjective wills, prevents the lovers' use of the forest as a strategy, a separate location in time and space within which to assert their autonomy.

Because Athenian society circumscribes and controls the forest, the fairies and the craftsmen directly serve the psychological and political needs not of the romantic or pastoral protagonists but of the primary-world ruling class: they help establish the relation between man and nature in such a way as to secure the authority of Theseus and Hippolyta over the complete range of Athenian civilization. Principally, the fairies serve the needs of the Athenian ruling class by their presupposition that nature certifies the hierarchical values, the dependence on degree and on the absolute subordination of subservients, on which the Duke's authority depends. The fairies repeat the Duke's values, his concern with authority, in an exaggerated form. Titania's court, especially, apotheosizes service and obediance: the Queen of the fairies is always accompanied by at least four attendants who solely function to envelop Titania with a protective circle of song and dance. The attendant fairies demonstrate pure service; they initiate no action whatever, but speak and act only in response to Titania's (and later, Bottom's) requests for action:

Come, now a roundel and a fairy song;
Then, for the third part of a minute, hence, . . . (II. ii. 1−2)

or:

> Nod to him, elves, and do him courtesies. (III. ii. 174)

In short, with their ritualistic chanting ("Ready./And I./And I./And I./Where shall we go?", III. ii. 163; "Hail, mortal!/ Hail!/Hail!/Hail!/", 175—8) they provide the fairy queen's court with a standard of adoring, even idolatrous, service to a central authority figure.

Obviously a more complex and spontaneous character, Puck serves the King of the fairies, perhaps as a court jester of sorts (II. i. 44), although he does not behave with such idolatry, with such dependence on his master's will. Puck, "that merry wanderer of the night", (II. i. 43) can act and judge independently; in fact, precisely because Oberon entrusts him with some autonomy he mistakes one Athenian for another. Puck's wanderings remain to an extent distinguished from those of the fairy whom he queries "whither wander you?" (1); the fairy's wanderings directly conjoin with his (her?) service to Titania:

> I do wander every where
> Swifter than the moon's sphere;
> And I serve the Fairy Queen,
> To dew her orbs upon the green. (II. i. 6—9)

But Puck's relative autonomy, by indirection, reinforces the theme of servility; his service to Oberon results not from the incapacity of his own personality but from a voluntary and a "natural" bond. Puck, enthusiastically, responds with complete subjection to each of Oberon's commands:

> I'll put a girdle round about the earth
> In forty minutes; (II. i. 175—6)

and:

> Fear not, my lord! your servant shall do so, (II. i. 268)

and:

I go, I go, look how I go,
Swifter than arrow from the Tartar's bow, (III. ii. 100–1)

and:

> Up and down, up and down,
> I will lead them up and down. (III. ii. 396–7)

In Shakespeare's works, the obvious analogue to Puck is Ariel, the spirit who performs supernatural feats at the bidding of an authority figure. But Ariel maintains a curious tension between enthusiastic service and the will to freedom; Puck never expresses that will, and is, therefore, in a surprising sense, closer to Caliban, who identifies freedom with service to a new master. Whereas *The Tempest* dramatizes Prospero's use of magic to impose his will on others, *A Midsummer Night's Dream* creates a vision of nature in which others do not or cannot resist impositions on their will: the ruling class projects its fantasies of mastery—or, more accurately, of devoted service—on to the forest spirits, who command obedience from their subordinates and who use the ecology of nature to control permanently the will of the romantic protagonists.

As their second function, also in some ways an obvious one, the fairies establish a cosmologic sympathy between the forces of nature and the actions and passions of the ruling class. On one level the turbulence in nature, which Titania describes—

> Therefore the winds, piping to us in vain,
> As in revenge, have suck'd up from the sea
> Contagious fogs; . . . (II. i. 88–114)

—seem to derive directly from the "forgeries of jealousy" (81) between Titania and Oberon:

> And this same progeny of evils comes
> From our debate, from our dissension;
> We are their parents and original. (II. i. 115–7)

The jealousy ostensibly concerns Titania's retention of a boy whom "jealous Oberon would have . . . / Knight of his train, to

trace the forests wild", (24– 5); the love Oberon and Titania have
for Hippolyta and Theseus also taints the jealousy:

Titania: Why art thou here
                    Come from the farthest steep of India?
                    But that, forsooth, the bouncing Amazon,
                    Your buskin'd mistress, and your warrior love,
                    To Theseus must be wedded, and you come
                    To give their bed joy and prosperity.
Oberon: How canst thou thus for shame, Titania,
                    Glance at my credit with Hippolyta,
                    Knowing I know thy love to Theseus? (II. i. 68– 76)

The suggestion of an erotic connection between the rulers of the
fairy world and the rulers of Athens transforms the fairies into
spiritual manifestations of the sexual drives of Theseus and
Hippolyta: Titania represents in the realm of spirit Theseus's
physical desire, held in abeyance during the four-day interval
before the wedding, for Hippolyta; Oberon represents Hippolyta's
desire for Theseus. The destructive jealousy with which Oberon
and Titania confront each other replaces, then, the injury, the
actual martial opposition between their two races, with which
Theseus "woo'd" Hippolyta. The correspondence of the discord
between Oberon and Titania to the disorder in nature has, by
extension, flattering and imperial implications for the fairies' mortal
counterparts, Theseus and Hippolyta: it implies that the conflict
between their nations disrupted the entire natural world, and,
further, that by introducing another "key", by bringing harmony
to their people through marriage, they can restore harmony and
order to the world of nature. Here, of course, Shakespeare
dramatizes or expresses one of the central concepts in the
"Elizabethan World Picture". The inclusion of the idea of
correspondence here in *A Midsummer Night's Dream* does not
mean, however, that Shakespeare took the picture at face value;
rather, it further indicates Shakespeare's understanding of the
strategies used by the ruling class to justify its power and its
retention of centralized authority through hypothetical analogy
with the forces of nature.

Whereas most versions of pastoral use the protagonists to
separate nature from the state, to find a life in nature independent

of hierarchic authority that characterizes the primary world, the presence in *A Midsummer Night's Dream* of the fairies as dominating forces within the forest completely dissolves the expected pastoral oppositions. Here, the state permeates and controls nature. The supposedly autonomous actions with which the romantic protagonists—and, in addition, Titania—express erotic desire come directly underneath control of the spiritual counterpart (Oberon) to the figure of authority in the state (Theseus). The predominant force in the play becomes not Theseus himself, but an aspect of Theseus, his spirit manifested in Oberon. The authoritarian principle, transformed into pure spirit, controls nature, uses nature to impose an order and direction on the seemingly irrational and preposterous behavior of the youthful Athenians. *A Midsummer Night's Dream* dissolves pastoral retreat and sexual rebellion into a ritualistic acceptance of the principle of authority; those released from Oberon's magical control submit to voluntary control by deferring to authoritarian predominance. Hippolyta, after relinquishing the changeling boy, takes hands in a stylized dance with Oberon (IV. i. 84–102); the Athenian lovers follow Theseus and Hippolyta "to the temple" (194–9). At the end of the play the lovers get what they wanted in the first place, but they do so in such a way as to confirm Theseus's authority and Oberon's capabilities: Theseus gets to "extenuate" the laws of Athens and to overbear Egeus' will; Oberon overbears Demetrius's will.

The complete predominance of Oberon, his instrumental role in bringing resolution to the dramatic antagonisms and oppositions, keeps nature separate not from the state but from those who cannot or will not submit to the supposedly "natural" forces of ruling-class authority. Nature, that is, joins with the state to transform retreat into an acquiesence to authority by imposing an order on the anarchic and apparently whimsical behavior of all of the lovers. Like the structure of the state, the imposed order is systemic: the "reasons" behind the erotic choices of the lovers do not appear to those who choose or are chosen, whereas to those on stage and in the audience who can see the entire system of choice—free will and enforced will—operating, the reasons for the particular choices and the motive for the imposition of such choices are evident. In isolation, the lovers' actions seem discordant: thus Puck considers "what fools these mortals be!" (III. ii. 115). As part of a system, the lovers' actions cohere into a strategy for authoritarian predominance over second-world consciousness and for transforming nature into an instrument of spirit. Through the ministrations of Puck, Oberon exercises exclusive power over nature and, consequently, over those living within nature. Because of his predominant control over nature, Oberon's (and Puck's) ritualistic language can bring about changes in the natural world, whereas the ritualistic language of others, both fairies and mortals, acts merely as rhetoric, decoration. For example, as soon as the fairies have completed their protective dance around the sleeping Titania:

> Chorus: Never harm,
>   Nor spell, nor charm,
>   Come our lovely lady nigh.
>   So good night, with lullaby,
>   . . .
> Second Fairy: Hence, away! Now all is well.
>   One aloof stand sentinel, (II. ii. 16– 19, 25– 6)

Oberon enters and imposes his spell on the lovely lady:

> What thou seest when thou dost wake,
> Do it for thy true-love take;
> Love and languish for his sake. (II. ii. 27– 9)

Similarly, as soon as Hermia and Lysander have finished their prayers:

> Hermia: good night, sweet friend.
>   Thy love ne'er alter till thy sweet life end!
> Lysander: Amen, amen, to that fair prayer, say I,
>   And then end life when I end loyalty!, (II. ii. 60– 3)

Puck enters and uses the natural herb in such a way that he completely negates the contents of the lovers' prayers.

The pastoral movement in *A Midsummer Night's Dream* demonstrates, then, that taking an active and independent role in relation to authority—either retreating to nature or expressing one's own nature through erotic love—places one in a subordinate position to the spiritual forces active within nature. The characters can only achieve their subjective desires and, in that sense, transcend social and legal restrictions, by submitting their wills to the predominant authority-figure in both the primary and second worlds. This movement includes the fantasy that one can act neither upon nature nor on the social structure that the hierarchy of nature justifies. The spirits within nature act upon and change— even physically transform—the characters; the characters become the objects of nature, and cannot become subjects who will change nature. All of those in opposition to the official will of authority find that they cannot use language, retreat, or physical force to impose their independent choices on the natural world: they resist the state in order to have their subjective wills reincorporated, through the agency of nature, into the will of the authority figure. Nature has a systemic correspondence to established human society, and as such it always resists the active human will to change.

Their enforced passive roles as objects of natural forces reduce the autonomy of the young aristocrats in order to reincorporate them, without resistance of their independent wills, into the ruling class. The passive relation to nature has the opposite effect, however, on the craftsmen: because nature has an autonomous and active role in regard to human society, the craftsmen are reduced in importance and kept carefully subordinate to the ruling class. By enacting their trades—carpenter, tailor, joiner, weaver, bellows-mender, tinker—the craftsmen ought ordinarily change or control nature, or, in the Marxist sense, create nature by bringing it within the control of human society and commerce. In *A Midsummer Night's Dream* the craftsmen are consciously separated from their crafts, in part because the play occurs during a proclaimed period of revelry. But in part the distinction between occupation and dramatic or aesthetic function helps us understand the significance and the use of nature in the play. The craftsmen, more than any of the other characters in the play, become and are treated as objects of nature: Puck refers to them, with a term unfortunately adopted by many critics, as "rude mechanicals", an epithet that objectifies the men and abstracts human skill from their work. Whereas nature manipulates the wills of the aristocrats and the fairy queen, it transforms Bottom's body; nature uses Bottom as a physical object, material substance for the fairy magic. Further, nature objectifies the others so as to serve their own erotic interests, whereas nature objectifies Bottom so as to use him in Oberon's plot against Titania. Bottom's transformation, that is, serves no end for Bottom himself, even though he experiences it after the fact as a mystical vision; Bottom's change serves only to facilitate the reconciliations of those with superior social status, the King and Queen of the fairies and, by correspondent extension, Theseus and Hippolyta.

Deprived of the technological control over nature implicit in their occupations, the craftsmen perform an abstract form of labor "in their minds" (V. i. 73); that is, they attempt to adopt the aristocratic attitude toward nature, to control violence and passion through the interpolation of the imagination, of rhetorical and verbal acts. Bottom, unwilling to "leave the killing out" of their play, declares:

> I have a device to make all well. Write me a prologue, and let the prologue seem to say we will do no harm with our swords, and that Pyramus is not kill'd indeed. . . . (III. i. 14, 16–19)

So that the ladies will not be "afeard of the lion", the actor who plays the part:

> must speak through, saying thus, or to the same defect: "Ladies," or "Fair ladies, I would wish you," or "I would request you", or "I would entreat you, not to fear, not to tremble: my life for yours." (III. i. 38–42)

Not only do the craftsmen attempt to replace violence with language, they plan to use language to re-create natural phenomena. Instead of bringing moonlight to their production by leaving "a casement of the great chamber window (where we play) open; and the moon may shine in at the casement", they decide that "one must come in with a bush of thorns and a lantern, and say he comes to disfigure, or to present, the person of Moonshine", (56–61).

Each verbal interpolation, although comic in itself, occurs within a social context from which we should not isolate it: within the boundaries of *A Midsummer Night's Dream*, the craftsmen only serve to entertain and to divert the aristocracy. Consequently one cannot speak of any relation established in the play between the craftsmen and nature independent of the relation, the relation of use, established between the craftsmen and either the Athenian aristocracy or its spirit counterparts. The hilarity of the craftsmen's ineffective attempts to control nature through language measures the craftsmen's dependence on aristocratic patronage: the play furthers the aristocracy's fantasy of its absolute social pre-dominance by replacing the craftsmen's physical control of nature in the performance of their work with their inept verbal control of nature in an artistic performance. This substitution removes from the craftsmen all of their implicit self-sufficiency as labourers and inverts the structure of the state: the state should depend on its foundation, those who work within the state and whose work creates the surplus and leisure time for those who rule. Here, with the craftsmen separated from the technical aspect of their work, they expect to thrive not on the objective, material products that they produce but on the pleasure that their aesthetic actions elicit from the aristocratic audience:

> If our sport had gone forward, we had all been made men. . . . O sweet bully Bottom! Thus hath he lost sixpence a day during his life; he could not have scap'd sixpence a day. And the Duke had not given him sixpence a day for playing Pyramus, I'll be hang'd. (IV. ii. 17–23)

The craftsmen can be "made men" only as a direct consequence of their subservience to the ruling class and of the suppression of their autonomy in the dramatic roles they play in "Pyramus and Thisbe".

The craftsmen, in effect, get incorporated into the ruling-class vision of society by exclusion from and reification by the ruling class. Correspondent to aristocratic fantasies that the spiritual world and the world of nature—the second world—confirm the hierarchical vision of society arises the fantasy that no actions taken within the primary world can have any intrinsic function or purpose, that all primary-world actions derive significance and motive from the need to offer service to the ruling class. In part the craftsmen themselves dramatize this fantasy through their un-mitigated devotion to the Duke, their yearning for patronage, and their fear of aristocratic authority:

> And you should do it too terribly, you would fright the Duchess

and the ladies, that they would shrike; and that were enough to hang us all.

That would hang us, every mother's son.

I grant you, friends, if you should fright the ladies out of their wits, they would have no more discretion but to hang us.

(I. ii. 74—81)

But primarily Duke Theseus's attitude toward the craftsmen dramatizes the fantasy. Because Theseus extends the boundaries of his ego so as to incorporate the craftsmen into his own consciousness, he deprives them of their autonomy and subjectivity. The famous passage in which Theseus expresses his magnanimous intention to "hear" "Pyramus and Thisbe" has a double edge:

Our sport shall be to take what they mistake;
And what poor duty cannot do, noble respect
Takes it in might, not merit.
Where I have come, great clerks have purposed
To greet me with premeditated welcomes;
Where I have seen them shiver and look pale,
Make periods in the midst of sentences,
Throttle their practic'd accent in their fears,
And in conclusion dumbly have broke off,
Not paying me a welcome. Trust me, sweet,
Out of this silence yet I pick'd a welcome. (V. i. 90—100)

As an isolated statement of intention, this passage indicates that rhetoric does not deceive Theseus, that for him meaning depends on the holistic quality of the presentation made by a speaker, clerk, orator, or actor. Theseus claims that he can determine the meaning of silence, can complete with his own consciousness the verbal acts of those who "dumbly have broke off". On one level, by picking a welcome out of silence Theseus confirms the deeper meaning of the great clerks by looking beneath the apparent ineptitudes of their surface utterances. On another level, looking beneath the surface utterance he disconfirms the authenticity of the speaker, denies that the speaker's words—or silences—have any meaning other than that which serves the social needs of the auditor.

Theseus's response to "Pyramus and Thisbe" dramatizes this disconfirmation. He reinterprets the blustering self-confidence of the craftsmen as "the modesty of fearful duty", (101) "tongue-tied simplicity", (104) and thus places the craftsmen in society solely as servants or subordinates to the ruling class. By announcing that he:

> will hear that play;
> For never any thing can be amiss,
> When simpleness and duty tender it, (V. i. 81−3)

Theseus disconfirms the aesthetic intentions of the craftsmen; he prejudges their competence and, in a sense, subordinates the intrinsic qualities of the craftsmen's aesthetic act to the needs of his ego. Theseus uses his imagination to appropriate the contents of the craftsmens' performance: he transforms their theatrical incompetence not just into the comic farce that the theatre-audience experiences but into his own capacity to elicit tribute and to inspire obedience. In fact the audience in the theatre, able to see both the craftsmen's performance and the aristocratic response to the performance, can see simultaneously enacted two kinds of disconfirmation and negation: the craftsmen negate the tragic contents of their play, decomposing the tragic materials of "Pyramus and Thisbe" into a hilariously comic performance, while the aristocrats, the on-stage audience, decompose the comic performance into a social tribute.

Not all of the aristocratic audience engages in this decomposition. Hermia and Helena remain demure; Hippolyta speaks primarily to challenge Theseus's appropriation. Hippolyta, in fact, appears in closest sympathy with the aesthetic intentions of the performers. Initially she does not want to see "Pyramus and Thisbe" because she fears the performers will embarrass themselves: "I love not to see wretchedness o'ercharged, /And duty in his service perishing", (85−6). Unlike Theseus, she will not substitute her imagination for the performers', or for the void left by what she perceives as the performers' lack of imagination:

Hippolyta: This is the silliest stuff that ever I heard.
Theseus: The best in this kind are but shadows; and the worst
    are no worse, if imagination amend them.
Hyppolyta: It must be your imagination then, and not theirs.

(V. i. 210−4)

Perhaps, however, because of her unwillingness to amend the performance with her own imagination—note that she says that it must be *your*, not *our*, imagination that will amend—Hippolyta, unlike Theseus, responds to the tragic materials of "Pyramus and Thisbe," to the intentions of the performers:

> Theseus: This passion, and the death of a dear friend, would go
> near to make a man look sad.
> Hippolyta: Beshrew my heart, but I pity the man.
> (V. i. 288–90)

This momentary split in the response of the on-stage audience suggests that the craftsmen's performance retains a residual competence. The performance itself, therefore, does not actually dramatize the differentiation between the two social groups; to some extent, as Hippolyta's resistance to Theseus shows, the magnanimous response of the aristocratic audience, the aristocracy's translation of the incompetence into "service", (81) results from their imaginative appropriation of the performance, from their *use* of the imagination rather than from the contents of the imaginative act performed before them. The audience response and re-creation, rather than the enactment itself, extend as far as possible the aristocratic autonomy as a social class.

Earlier, the aristocratic imagination had incorporated rebellion against authority into a ritual celebration of its own power; here the aristocracy uses imagination to enforce an absolute split within the working—redefined as serving—class into subject and object. Because the audience treats the craftsmen as objects, as "hard-handed" (72) men without feelings and without purpose other than service to the ruling class, the product of their service, the artistic performance, becomes completely subjective, devoid of meaning until informed by the aristocratic imagination. The enforced split allows the aristocrats to incorporate the subjective aspect of the craftsmen into their own consciousnesses, as part of their own artistic imaginations. At the same time, the aristocrats apply a careful distinction between their own subjectivity as individuals with feelings and their objective vision of the craftsmen as oblivious performers, segments of the courtly landscape.

HARMONY

Almost all critics who have written about *A Midsummer Night's Dream* have argued that the play concludes with restored harmony, with concord achieved out of discord, with an emphasis on variety, balance, or reconciled contrasts.[5] Each of these phrases—the differences among them are not really so great—presupposes a criticism that abstracts the emotional, tonal, structural, or modal quality of the play from the social relations and oppositions dramatized within the play. Abstract criticism tends to treat the "words" of the play as terms that can be arranged or balanced against one another so as to create harmonic effects or patterns. By seeing the worlds as separate and separable terms, abstract criticism deprives each class or group of characters of its material social existence and replaces the transforming, dialectical relations that determine the relations between social classes with the static conception of a conventional social order. Peter F. Fisher, for example, argues that, at the end of the play, the dialectics of Puck restores harmony, but note what, for him, harmony consists of:

> [The] world of reason and accepted order is seated with Theseus and Hippolyta in the place of honor and power; that of passion and desire is once more firmly within the orbit of rational influence and control; and the world of common life and activity disports itself for their amusement and approval. The world of imagination and fantasy remains the undercurrent which ends the play.[6]

This system constitutes harmony only for those with "influence and control"; for others, the conclusion may contain tension and discord. By keeping each of these worlds separate and equal and by accepting the suppression of one social class as "conventional", Fisher's criticism subverts the central social issue in the play, the strategy through which the ruling class maintains its autonomy, to the abstraction "harmony". He thereby abstracts the resolution of the play from the social relations and class fantasies that produced that particular *form* of resolution.

Other critics impose on or abstract from the play a pattern, which allows them to ignore the social condition of those who act within the pattern and of those who create the pattern. G. K. Hunter is most straightforward about this particular method. He calls *A Midsummer Night's Dream* a suite of dances "seeking to reconcile, without judging, the comparative merits of the different worlds that are shown", and he argues that the play concerns the "pattern", not the individuals who compose the pattern. This abstraction allows Hunter to argue that the "ignorance of the mechanicals" functions primarily to contrast with the "innocence" of the young lovers, to make their innocence into a relative virtue. The pattern that Hunter abstracts from the play therefore enables him to ignore the social and intellectual conditions of one class of characters except in so far as these conditions help the audience sympathize with the aristocratic protagonists.[7] Blaize Odell Bonazza, similarly, abstracts a "structure" from *A Midsummer Night's Dream* and finds that the play exemplifies an "ideal" four-plot, "multi-level structure". By separating the social elements in the play into distinct levels of plot that join at the conclusion, Bonazza can find in Act V a "balanced society . . . composed of reconciled contrasts between reason and passion and the rescinded inclusion of instinct".[8] The structural balance, when reapplied to the play in terms of social relations, of course, presupposes an identification of classes with distinct levels, and, by definition, levels with height or stature. The multi-level structure in *A Midsummer Night's Dream* implies that only when one class attains the "highest" (a "serious, enveloping action") and another the "lowest" ("anti-romantic parody") structural level, society is balanced and contrast is reconciled.

Probably the most common form of critical abstraction about *A Midsummer Night's Dream*, and perhaps about all of Shakespeare's comedies, occurs when critics substitute the general concept *society* for the class-bound vision of society that the conclusion of the play enforces. Particularly those critics influenced by Northrop Frye's archetypal methods exercise this form of abstraction. James E. Robinson, who has made the most extensive application of modal criticism to *A Midsummer Night's Dream*, argues that the world of ritual, from its context of nature and divinity, subsumes the social or "rhetorical" problems in the play. He writes that "the main structure of the play" designedly bypasses "the specific problems of custom and law" and takes the Athenian lovers "through a magical and transcendent experience", (387). Robinson argues

that by "participation in ritual" *A Midsummer Night's Dream*
"elevates" society "into the comic mythos of renewal in communion with nature and its gods", (391).[9] As soon as we note the
objectification of the craftsmen, and the servile, inferior position to
which they are relegated at the conclusion, we realize that not
"society", but only a class within society, has access to communion
with nature, etc. The comic mythos depends on a maintained class
differentiation. To argue that the comic renewal bypasses specific
social problems implies the belief that a society in which one class
maintains subjective autonomy while another is relegated to
servile objectivity is not a problem.

Paradoxically, those few critics who note an absence of social
problems in *A Midsummer Night's Dream* come closest to discover-
ing the actual nature of the social problems that the play develops.
Barber, for one, notes that in *A Midsummer Night's Dream*
"mastery comes a little too easily",[10] that Shakespeare too easily
develops "polarities" and allows Theseus to "box off" holiday
from everyday reality (p. 161). Sheldon P. Zitner, similarly, argues
that, in *A Midsummer Night's Dream*, the characters avoid sinister
overtones, moral implications, and the usual complications implicit in romantic materials and that the play becomes a "pure"
comedy, a "drama of avoidance" that offers "an easy access to the
good old disappearing Ways", (402–3).[11] Barber and Zitner
advance beyond abstract criticism in that they both detect an
element of fantasy, wish-fulfillment, and improbability in the
dramatic resolution. Neither critic, however, suggests either that
the fantasy has a class content or that the drama *contains* the fantasy,
that is, that *A Midsummer Night's Dream* does not act as a fantasy for
its audience but dramatizes the aristocratic fantasy of, and strategy
for, creating complete social poise.

The success of the fantasy, of the aristocratic use of the
imagination in order to achieve harmony within nature and
separation from those who work with the materials of nature,
represents an extreme point in Shakespeare's comedies, or even in
this particular comedy. The sense of social poise with which
Theseus ushers the Athenians off the stage partially gets dissolved
by the contents and implications of the blessings with which the
fairies conclude the play, with which they "sweep the dust behind
the door", (V. i. 390). Puck's benediction restores to the play an
awareness of the oppositions both between the ruling class and

nature and between the ruling class and labour, an awareness that the aristocratic fantasies of autonomy have worked to suppress:

> Now the hungry [lion] roars,
> And the wolf [behowls] the moon;
> Whilst the heavy plowman snores,
> All with weary task foredone.
> Now the wasted brands do glow,
> Whilst the screech-owl, screeching loud,
> Puts the wretch that lies in woe
> In remembrance of a shroud. (V. i. 371–8)

Puck's speech evokes not only the real dangers of nature—*real* lions and wolves—but also the real hardships of physical labour. This emphasis on physical danger and hardship suggests a world outside of or beyond the palace threshold, a world of nature that the aristocratic imagination cannot thoroughly subordinate. Oberon's ambiguous blessing of the bride-beds extends and confirms this sense of the dangers implicit in nature:

> And the blots in Nature's hand
> Shall not in their issue stand;
> Never mole, hare-lip, nor scar,
> Nor mark prodigious, such as are
> Despised in nativity,
> Shall upon their children be. (V. i. 409–14)

The contents of Oberon's blessing work against Oberon's declared intent: the feeling of deformity and dis-ease that his words establish predominates over the condition of "safety" (420) that his blessing proclaims. The tensions and ambiguity that Oberon's blessing contains make manifest, right at the conclusion of the play, both the success and the incapacities of the aristocratic strategy. Just as Oberon's language both creates a problem then wishes it away, the aristocratic use of the imagination acknowledges oppositions both within the aristocracy and between the aristocracy and other classes, then wishes those problems and oppositions away through the disconfirmation of others' autonomy.

The element of fantasy, however, circumscribes the feeling of danger that predominates at the conclusion: the spirit of the forest describes "the blots in Nature's hand" in order to offer protection therefrom. In effect, then, *A Midsummer Night's Dream* ends by incorporating nature, with its attendant sense of danger, within the Athenian society: the forces of nature certify and bless the aristocratic predominance and autonomy. Shakespeare's later comedies will develop by reversing the contents of this conclusion: whereas *A Midsummer Night's Dream* concludes as the implicit hierarchy in nature joins the Athenian society, in the later comedies the aristocrats will extend their vision of an established hierarchical society outward, into the uncivil world of nature.

4 *As You Like It*

"YOUR GRACE, THAT CAN TRANSLATE"

Rosalind and Celia state, "in sport," the opposition that, taken in earnest, becomes the initial, primary-world problem in *As You Like It*:

> Celia: Let us sit and mock the good huswife Fortune from her wheel, that her gifts may henceforth be bestow'd equally.
> Rosalind: I would we could do so; for her benefits are mightily misplac'd, and the bountiful blind woman doth most mistake in her gifts to women. (I. ii. 31–6)

We cannot tell whether Rosalind refers to women in general, or to herself and Celia as two women in particular. Surely the opposition between Rosalind's own bad fortune, "a banish'd father" (5–6), and Celia's good fortune illustrates the unequal distribution of Fortune's gifts to women. But Celia tactfully shifts their discussion to women in general:

> 'Tis true, for those she makes fair she scarce makes honest, and those that she makes honest she makes very ill-favoredly. (I. ii. 37–9)

Celia's comment, which presumably has no particular relevance for herself and Rosalind, does allow Rosalind to make a general observation and to amend and expand the terminology of their discussion. Rosalind suggests that whereas oppositions within the species (some women have good fortune, others do not) can be attributed solely to Fortune, oppositions within the individual (some women are fair but dishonest, others are honest but ill-

70

favoured) must be attributed to an antonymic opposition between Fortune and Nature:

> Nay, now thou goest from Fortune's office to Nature's. Fortune reigns in the gifts of the world, not in the lineaments of Nature. (I. ii. 40–2)

Rosalind uses this Nature/Fortune opposition to distinguish between what we can call essence and accident: Nature is fixed, unchanging, and, in a sense, initial or primary; Fortune is mutable, secondary or consequential, and, in a sense, concerns event rather than character. Celia illustrates:

> when Nature hath made a fair creature, may she not by Fortune fall into the fire? Though Nature hath given us wit to flout at Fortune, hath not Fortune sent in this fool to cut off the argument? (I. ii. 43–7)

The Nature/Fortune opposition, then, does more than expand the terminology of Rosalind and Celia's discussion; by redefining the inequity of Fortune, it also suggests an entirely different method for remedial action. Now Fortune stands accused not of unequal distribution of her gifts but of lack of harmony with Nature. *Some* of the inequities of Fortune are thereby justified: inasmuch as Rosalind and Celia do not question the so-called natural differences among people, flouting at Fortune need no longer contain an implicit plea for equalization. Their discussion only advocates a reconciliation of one's fortune with one's "natural" condition or deserts.

The scene preceding Rosalind and Celia's discussion, the first scene of *As You Like It*, dramatizes the opposition between Nature and Fortune, and in such a way as to decry explicitly Orlando's bad fortune but to accept implicitly a "naturally" determined differentiation of social conditions in general, or in the species. Orlando opens *As You Like It* by complaining to Adam that the conditions and opportunities of his life do not match his natural gifts, the conditions into which and the qualities with which he was born. Orlando himself does not recognize a distinction between conditions and qualities; his references to his birth and to nature confuse and combine—as have most readers—the conditions of his class with his physical and spiritual qualities as an individual:

> he [Oliver] keeps me rustically at home, or (to speak more
> properly) stays me here at home unkept; for call you that
> keeping for a gentleman of my birth, that differs not from the
> stalling of an ox?, (I. i. 7–11)

and:

> Besides this nothing that he so plentifully gives me, the
> something that nature gave me his countenance seems to take
> from me. He lets me feed with his hinds, bars me the place of a
> brother, and as much as in him lies, mines my gentility with my
> education. This is it, Adam, that grieves me, and the spirit of my
> father, which I think is within me, begins to mutiny against this
> servitude. (I. i. 16–24)

Orlando's complaint, in effect, opens the play with an attack on his
own bad fortune, but he keeps the attack on Fortune within the
oppositional confine, Fortune versus Nature, that Rosalind will
later enunciate. Contained, Orlando's attack on Fortune, on his
condition, fails to move beyond the individual case: although *his*
fortune does not suit his nature, Orlando's outburst contains no
awareness that the rustics and "hinds", with whom he is kept and
fed, also suffer from the effects of Fortune. By implication, the
servitude in which the hinds are kept suits their nature, just as the
ox is suited to its "stalling"; the mutiny against servitude has
nothing to do with the condition of servitude itself, but only with
the nature of the one kept in service.

   The Nature/Fortune opposition, then, does not exactly work as
a general social problem in *As You Like It*; rather, through this
opposition members of the ruling class identify their particular,
individual problems. Rosalind and Orlando, notably, use the
opposition to identify their own misfortunes in such a way that
their attempts to rectify the effects of Fortune will not remedy the
misfortune of those in other social classes, unfortunate by, or
because of, their "nature". The Nature/Fortune opposition
protects the ruling class from the revolutionary, or at least the
"levelling", implications of its attack on Fortune, on immediate
social conditions. But attack, of course, inaccurately explains the

actions of the mis-fortunate aristocrats. Although, as John Shaw
has pointed out, the permanence of Nature and the mutability of
Fortune necessarily correlate with the Nature/Fortune opposition,[1] which implies that one can reconcile the Nature/Fortune
opposition only by altering one's fortune, the ruling class in *As You
Like It* seems peculiarly discouraged from or incapable of a direct
attack on Fortune. Only two characters, Duke Frederick and
Oliver, attempt to change their fortunes, to act directly within
rather than flee from the realm of Fortune: they banish and confine
their rival brothers. The whole tone of the play, however, censures
their actions, and both, late in the play, are reconciled to a passive
acceptance of the conditions of life, an acceptance that the play
seems to advocate. Rosalind and, especially, Orlando have more
justification for acting within the realm of Fortune, but both
appear to be incapable of such action. When Orlando, for
example, asks his brother for the money left him by their father,
with which he hopes to "buy" his "fortunes", Oliver silences him
by reminding him of his incapacity for constructive action: "And
what wilt thou do? beg, when that is spent?" (I. i. 75—6). Orlando
later confirms his own incapacity; when Adam warns him that he
must not return to his home, he laments:

> What, wouldst thou have me go and beg my food?
> Or with a base and boist'rous sword enforce
> A thievish living on the common road?
> This I must do, or know not what to do;
> Yet this I will not do, do how I can. (II. iii. 31—5)

Rosalind, although not as directly, acknowledges the same
incapacity; she challenges Fortune through memory, or through
forgetting:

> Dear Celia . . . Unless you could teach me to forget a banish'd
> father, you must not learn me to remember any extraordinary
> pleasure.
> . . . .
> Well, I will forget the condition of my estate, to rejoice in yours.
> (I. ii. 3—7, 15—16)

This incapacity to act within the realm of Fortune, or the

unseemliness of an aristocrat's doing so, results from the aristocracy's assumption that Nature itself, through its supposedly stable and hierarchic structure, justifies and secures aristocratic autonomy and social station. Although in a sense their inability to take direct action so as to restore their fortunes restricts both Rosalind and Orlando, in a more profound sense the passive reliance on, or faith in, the resilience of their aristocratic natures, the "spirit" within them, protects them from the mutability of Fortune. Having perceived as a problem not the mutability of Fortune but the opposition between Fortune and Nature, the protagonists in *As You Like It* propose as a solution that particular form of action most protective of their prerogatives as members of the ruling class. Were the protagonists to oppose misfortune by placing faith in Fortune, by taking remedial action such as resisting Duke Frederick's usurped or Oliver's misused authority, they would in a sense endorse the very forces that have displaced them: they would acknowledge that Nature has not fixed one's social station, but that some people can restore social station through direct action. Carried a step further, such an endorsement of the interdependence of Fortune and social station would, by implication, suggest that one is born into the ruling, and not some other, class merely by good fortune, and that, just as action can restore the social station lost through misfortune, Fortune can diminish even the so-called "natural" social station into which one was born. Consequently, rather than reconciling Nature with Fortune by trying to change their misfortunes, and thereby facing the consequences of dependence on Fortune, the protagonists reconcile the opposition by retreat to the unchanging forest, the condition of Nature.

Admittedly, the natural world to which the aristocratic protagonists retreat differs to some extent from the Nature that they have opposed to Fortune. With help from the invaluable set of definitions of *nature* enumerated by Arthur O. Lovejoy and George Boas,[2] we can distinguish between the two different and divergent "Natures" that *As You Like It* dramatizes. The one is Nature as:

Definition 8. The permanent and fundamental character of a
person, in contrast with transient manifestations
or superficial appearances,

or:

Definition 9. The intrinsic and permanent quality or qualities
of (physical) things;

the other "Nature" is:

Definition 17. The antithesis of . . . "culture" or "art"; . . . a
generic or collective name for that which arises
without human effort or contrivance, in contrast with that which man produces through his
purposive action,

and, by extension:

Definition 32. The out-of-doors.

But in part *As You Like It* unites these divergent definitions, or uses,
of *nature*. As many critics, among them notably John Russell
Brown, have observed, the Forest of Arden mirrors one's mind;[3]
but this mirror-effect, I think, results not so much from the forest as
from the mind. In Arden the protagonists experience the formation of delusions as described by Freud: feelings and internal
processes appear as if they were "the consequences of an external
perception", "what was abolished internally, returns from without".[4] Just as Jaques has his own melancholy returned to him by
the "sobbing" deer, in the Forest of Arden Nature as an "intrinsic
quality" (Definition 9) appears as or is expressed by the external
qualities of Nature as "the out-of-doors" (Definition 32). In the
forest, appearances express "permanent and fundamental characteristics" but the appearances are not the "transient manifestations
and superficial appearances" opposed to *nature* in Definition 8;
rather, they are the permanent and profound appearances that
themselves also constitute *nature*, as in Definition 32.

In the Forest of Arden, then, Nature (Definition 32) expresses
Nature (Definitions 8, 9), and, thus, the gap between internal and
external, or self and other, closes and disappears. The subjectivity
of the protagonists merges with the objective conditions of the
environment. This resolution, however, depends on a particular
hierarchy of the definitions of *nature*: the protagonists do not

perceive themselves, their own intrinsic qualities, as encompassed by or in terms of the out-of-doors; rather, they see the out-of-doors in their own terms: in short, they project. They therefore subordinate the out-of-doors to human needs and conditions, they stylize Nature. In a process typical of pastoral literature, the Nature to which the protagonists retreat becomes, according to the antitheses in Definition 17, its own opposite; the characters produce Nature, they re-create Nature as a style: Nature becomes art. Duke Senior's often-quoted speech, which introduces us to Arden, clearly illustrates the predominant pastoral tendency to see Nature in cultural or artistic terms:

> Here feel we not the penalty of Adam,
> The seasons' difference, as the icy fang
> And churlish chiding of the winter's wind,
> Which when it bites and blows upon my body
> Even till I shrink with cold, I smile and say,
> "This is no flattery: these are counsellors
> That feelingly persuade me what I am." (II. i. 5—11)

As some critics have noted, the Duke perceives Nature as a linguistic act.[5] The physical conditions of his world work upon him stylistically and rhetorically, chide and persuade him. This linguistic quality that the Duke attributes to, or we might say creates in, his world, then becomes even more explicit:

> And this our life, exempt from public haunt,
> Finds tongues in trees, books in the running brooks,
> Sermons in stones, and good in every thing. (II. i. 15—7)

By the end of the Duke's speech, Nature no longer has merely some of the qualities of language, such as the ability to persuade; the Duke has redefined Nature as fundamentally verbal, containing within itself tongues, books, and sermons. The Duke has transformed Nature into style.

Amiens's response to Duke Senior, however, suggests or brings to the surface a different transformation process:

> Happy is your Grace,
> That can translate the stubbornness of fortune
> Into so quiet and so sweet a style. (II. i. 18—20)

The Duke has also "translated" Fortune; in fact, as Robert Pierce has pointed out, the ambiguous qualities of the verb *translate* identify Fortune even before the Duke had worked upon it as a "language", material for translation. According to Amiens's statement, which the play as a whole supports, the Duke's passive acceptance of Fortune actually negates Fortune. Merely by having labelled the usurpation as "the stubbornness of fortune" the Duke and his followers have translated Fortune into style: the Duke's banishment does not result from a human action, something that can be resisted with other actions, but from something beyond direct human control, which therefore invites only passive contemplation and acceptance. Having seen Duke Frederick's mind and policies in action, the audience, by the beginning of Act II, knows that more than Fortune has determined Duke Senior's banishment, but by abstracting Duke Frederick's role in the usurpation, Amiens—an official spokesman here—divorces the political consequences from their human agent and thereby treats both conditions, banishment and pastoral retreat, as styles, the one translatable into the other.

By translating banishment into Fortune, Fortune into style, the exiled courtiers have done more, however, than negate the necessity for action. Perhaps surreptitiously (thus exemplifying what William Empson would call one of the "tricks" of pastoral), they have also resolved the opposition between Fortune and Nature by creating a common denominator for the two terms. Because in the Forest of Arden the protagonists translate both Fortune and Nature into style, they can treat the two terms as if they were equivalent, as if they could be converted into each other. As a much more voluntary and subjective, and as a humanly created ("that which man produces through his purposive action", see Definition 17) quality, style gives the protagonists the feeling, or illusion, that they control the external, objective forces of Fortune and Nature. As a consequence, the protagonists use style to express, as the predominant aspect of both Fortune and Nature, their own subjective treatment of or reaction to these external phenomena, rather than the innate qualities of the phenomena, rather than the effect the external phenomena have on the subject.

We see this process enacted in the first Arden scene. The Duke not only translates nature into style and negates the antithesis between Nature and humanly created culture or art (Definition

17), but also appropriates Nature as the occasion for his style. The Duke does not feel the physical effects of nature ("Here feel we not the penalty of Adam, /The seasons' difference") except as "counsellors that feelingly persuade" him what he is: the climate becomes a verbal replication of a court, but here a court that defines and asserts the Duke's identity. From the ecology of the forest, the objective conditions of Nature, the Duke abstracts specific properties—the seasons' difference, trees, brooks, stones—from which he can construct a style and a subjective response. The properties of Nature thereby become a groundwork for the Duke's stylistic formulations. The Duke's presence in Arden disrupts the sense of an organic, mutual dependence that binds the things of Nature to one another; the Duke and his followers perceive or "use" Nature by separating its properties from one another and then, rather than trying to articulate a systemic relation among the parts of their environment (as Corin, for example, does regarding his environment: "good pasture makes fat sheep" etc, III. ii. 27), they comment on the isolated part through a series of stylistic abstractions, which effectively shifts the dramatic focus from the properties of Nature to the conditions of human culture and the quality of the speaker's literary style.

The "sobbing deer" episode nicely exemplifies this process of stylistic abstraction from the conditions of Nature. The Duke suggests that he and his followers "go and kill" venison; then he comments on his own suggestion:

> And yet it irks me the poor dappled fools,
> Being native burghers of this desert city,
> Should in their own confines with forked heads
> Have their round haunches gor'd. (II. i. 21–5)

We would be hard pressed to find a more mannered speech elsewhere in Shakespeare's works. Part of the mannerism results from the Duke's artful use of the passive voice: he is not irked that he must gore the round haunches of the dappled fools, but that the fools should—by some abstract, unnamed force (i.e. not the Duke's followers)—"have their round haunches gored". Further, the Duke uses rhetorical strategies, notably anthropomorphism (fools, burghers) and synecdoche (forked heads for arrows, round haunches for deer), to avoid naming the object or victim of his contemplation. As a result, the speech directs its auditors to contemplate neither the condition of the deer nor their own relation to their environment; the speech, rather, moves from the initial "go and kill" in a process of abstraction that by drawing attention to its language protects the auditors from contemplation of the language referent, the deer.

The process of abstraction, which moves from the deer to the Duke's feelings about the deer, continues as an attendant lord, responding to the Duke, abstracts the discussion a step further to the Duke's feelings about another's (Jaques's) feelings about the deer. Contemplating the condition of a wounded deer, Jaques could have been, if presented on stage, a mirror of the Duke's own sentiments; instead, the play presents Jaques's feelings at one remove: although Jaques moralized the spectacle of the sobbing deer, the lord gives us—or the Duke—a spectacle that includes Jaques himself. The Duke's interest in the condition of the deer, of man's disruptive effect on nature, now barely includes the deer at all, but centres on Jaques and on Jaques's translation of nature into style:

Duke Senior: But what said Jaques?
          Did he not moralize this spectacle?
1. Lord: O yes, into a thousand similes. (II. i. 43—5)

Jaques's moralizing approximates the Duke's initial insight; Jaques swears that the courtiers:

Are mere usurpers, tyrants, and what's worse,
To fright the animals and to kill them up
In their assign'd and native dwelling-place. (II. i. 61—3)

But the Duke, kept at a distance both by Jaques's rhetorical posturing and by the Lord's narrative account, can now bypass the anxiety he had expressed initially and can submerge his feelings about the condition of the deer in his joyful anticipation of a discussion with the person contemplating the deer: "I love to cope him in these sullen fits, /For then he's full of matter", (67—8). These processes of abstraction and of stylistic embellishment protect the Duke, and perhaps his followers as well, from the harshness and violence of their aggressive relation to the natural environment.

The effectiveness of the second-world strategy in *As You Like It* depends on the protagonists' ability to use style in this protective way, not just to protect themselves against cognizance of their disruptive position in Nature, but also to protect themselves against cognizance of their conflicts with a culture. Through recourse to style, the protagonists assert and maintain an autonomy, and thus they remain free, as subjects, from the determining, oppositional forces both of Nature and of Fortune, as mediated through human action. Rosalind and Celia's retreat to the forest aptly demonstrates how style protects the protagonists from the stubbornness of Fortune. Banished by the usurping Duke Frederick, the two women "devise" (I. iii. 100, 135) a plan for escape to the Forest of Arden, much as they had agreed, earlier, to "devise sports" (I. ii. 24–5). As they plan to leave for Arden, Rosalind's banishment quickly becomes the occasion for both women to formulate a playful costume drama: before they have considered "the fittest time and safest way /To hide [themselves] from pursuit that will be made" (I. iii. 135–6), they have already selected roles, costumes, props, and pseudonyms, and they have agreed to take along the court fool for their diversion. Clearly, they give prominence to the adventurous, imaginative, and playful aspects of their retreat so as to avoid active recognition of, or to divert Rosalind's incipient discussion of, the pain of leaving home and the dangers they might face when travelling. In short, they convert actual "banishment" and self-exile into an expected "liberty" (138).

The liberty that they create depends, however, more on process than on completion, more on transition than on arrival. Although Celia initially proposed that they "fly" the court intending "to seek" Duke Senior "in the forest of Arden" (100, 107), once she and Rosalind arrive in Arden they no longer seek the Duke. In fact, the disguises, which they originally devised in order to protect themselves and to facilitate their safe passage to the exiled court, become, once they arrive in the forest, a protection against being incorporated into the Duke's society, against being recognized by the Duke. Rosalind herself says, in a passage that troubles many critics:

I met the Duke yesterday, and had much question with him. He ask'd me of what parentage I was. I told him of as good as he, so he laugh'd and let me go. But what talk we of fathers, when there is such a man as Orlando? (III. iv. 35—9)

This behavior hardly seems consistent with one who first appears in the play with:

I show more mirth than I am mistress of, and would you yet [I] were merrier? Unless you could teach me to forget a banish'd father, you must not learn me how to remember any extraordinary pleasure. (I. ii. 3—7)

This change in Rosalind's behavior indicates more than a shift in emotional allegiance from her father to her "child's father", (I. iii. 10—11). Her unwillingness to speak with her father, or, in positive terms, her desire to remain in male disguise, exemplifies the same second-world strategy that the Duke himself has practiced. Were Rosalind to join her father in the forest and thus supply a terminus to her flight from the court, she would transform her exile into a process of running away from the authority of Duke Frederick. Rosalind does not acknowledge and verify the actual political power that Duke Frederick has over her life; rather, she translates her exile into a life that feels as if it were voluntarily chosen and whose rudiments and conditions can be determined solely by her own will. Like her father, she treats Duke Frederick's political actions as the stubbornness of Fortune so as to translate Fortune into a style.

So, although Rosalind remains in disguise long after the practical need for the disguise has passed, her disguise serves needs other than the practical. As a form of style, disguise allows her to feel and to act as if she controls her own emotions and the emotions of others. These qualities, the simultaneous participation and detachment for which so many have praised the character of Rosalind, do not so much distinguish a unique personality for Rosalind as they associate Rosalind's actions with the actions of the other protagonists. Duke Senior gains precisely the same effect by translating his exile, over which he has no control, into a style, which he does control. Consequently, we should not try to see Rosalind's particular style, the feigned homosexual courtship of Orlando, as a process through which she actually controls her own and others' fortunes; she uses style, rather, to translate her total lack of control into the feeling or illusion of complete control.

By this I mean that the motive for Rosalind's particular style of courting Orlando really has nothing to do with Orlando himself, nor with Rosalind's feelings toward him; Rosalind does not, as has often been argued, use disguise primarily to test Orlando's love or to educate him about love. Certainly the gaping wonder with which Orlando ultimately receives Rosalind ("If there be truth in sight, you are my Rosalind", V. iv. 119—his last words in the play) indicates that the courtship has confirmed rather than purged Orlando's idealization and over-valuation of Rosalind's powers; certainly Rosalind could most effectively have tested Orlando's love by offering him as the alternative to the "absent" Rosalind not a boy playing Rosalind but an eligible woman— Celia/Aliena.[6] In fact, however, Rosalind's maintenance of the disguise, and particularly of the homosexual bearing of the disguise, stylistically embellishes her courtship of Orlando. The stylized courtship serves a psychodynamic function concerning Rosalind's relation to the court of Duke Frederick. Rosalind's homosexual courtship precisely reverses the process of paranoid delusional formation that Freud describes. According to Freud's account, the delusion of persecution (paranoia) arises as a defense against homosexual feelings: the proposition "I (a man) love him" gets denied and negated into "I hate him", which in turn:

> becomes transformed by projection into . . . "He *hates* (persecutes) *me*, which will justify me in hating him." And thus the impelling unconscious feeling makes its appearance as though it were the consequence of an external perception.[7]

Rosalind, however, takes advantage of the interchangeability of the fathers in *As You Like It* ("But is all this for your father? No, some of it is for my child's father," I. iii. 10–11; "Wilt thou change fathers? I will give thee mine," I. iii. 91) and fuses the two "him's" (Duke Frederick and Orlando) to deny not the delusion of persecution but *real* persecution. Rosalind negates the proposition "He (Duke Frederick) hates me" by creating a homosexual feeling, thus: "He does not hate me, he (Orlando) loves me, and therefore I (a man) can love him." The style that she creates, the feigned homosexual courtship of Orlando, keeps her from experiencing as persecution the actions of her antagonist, Duke Frederick.

Although Rosalind uses style as a protection, so long as her style remains bound to the disguised courtship of Orlando, it cannot resolve the initial problem that confronted Rosalind. The subjective, psychodynamic strategy that she creates works for her, but does not work upon the objective, material conditions of her world: her homosexual style leaves Duke Frederick's tyranny and Duke Senior's banishment intact. In order to respond to the real, primary-world persecution, Rosalind must give her subjective style its own real, objective status in a new environment; she must use her subjectivity to "create", as her father has done, a second world. To do so, Rosalind must project the control that her disguise enables her to feel out into the world, so that the internal feeling of control can return to her from without, be expressed *to* her through social relations. When Rosalind's style becomes objective, gets returned to her by another source, it appears that she has created a world based on the conditions and prerogatives of her own style, a second world, and that she thereby has negated the stubbornness of Fortune and reconciled her individual fortune with her own intrinsic nature.

Rosalind accomplishes this feat, removes herself from the limitations of her own disguise, by projecting her style and her control of others onto the figure of Hymen. In the last scene of *As You Like It*, Rosalind's style expands into ritual; she gives up her disguise to gain a wider and more profound control, no longer only over her courtship of Orlando, but now over the entire pastoral society. While still disguised as the boy Ganymed, and thus containing her own style, Rosalind claims to have "promis'd to make all this matter even", (V. iv. 18) and she repeats the phrase as she departs from the stage: "and from hence I go /To make these doubts all even" (24–5). Rosalind returns to the stage, however, with her style split apart: she reappears *in propria persona*, but accompanied by "a person representing Hymen" (*Dramatis Personae*). This Hymen, presumably then a figure in disguise, claims to have taken on Rosalind's controlling or restorative functions, once more repeating Rosalind's phrasing:

> Then is there mirth in heaven
> When earthly things made even
>   Atone together.

> Good Duke, receive thy daughter,
> Hymen from heaven brought her,
>   Yea, brought her hither, . . . (V. iv. 108–13)

We experience a complex, ambiguous reaction here. Rosalind
at once designates her control to someone else or to some other
force, and at the same time increases our sense of the extent of her
control. We hear that Hymen, not Rosalind, "must make
conclusion/Of these most strange events" (126–7), yet by
allowing her feeling of control to return to her from without,
Rosalind expands our sense of her capacity to control, for we also
know that Hymen constitutes a part of the ritualistic style by
which Rosalind concludes the courtship she had begun as
Ganymed. Further, by designating the resolution that we know
she herself has created to the power of Hymen, Rosalind creates
the illusion or the feeling that the "strange events" of the
conclusion could not have taken place without heavenly intervention. The presence of Hymen, and the formal, ritualistic,
incantatory language that he speaks and seems to inspire in others:

> Duke Senior: O my dear niece, welcome, thou art to me,
>   Even daughter, welcome, in no less degree.
> Phebe: I will not eat my word, now thou art mine,
>   Thy faith my fancy to thee doth combine
> (V. iv. 147–50)

—draws attention to itself as style, distracting us from the
particular contents of the dramatic resolution: Rosalind appears to
her father and to Orlando, which she could have elected to do at
any time since arriving in Arden, and Phebe must "accord" herself
to Sylvius (133), which could, as in *Twelfth Night*, be attributed to
"Nature" drawing "to her bias" (*T. N.*, V. i. 260). Consequently,
Rosalind's control, when returned to her from without by means
of the exaggerated style of ritual, reappears in magnified form: the
events that Rosalind finally allows to occur seem "supernatural",
much more mysterious and difficult than they would have without
Hymen's presence.

The surprising entry of Jaques de Boys, which really concludes
the strange events in the forest, confirms and expands rather than
resolves the ambiguity of the conclusion that Rosalind arranged

and staged. Rosalind's conclusion felt ambiguous because while it attributed her real control of events to another force, it exaggerated our sense of the importance and difficulty of the events that were controlled. Jaques de Boys's announcement sustains this ambiguity, but with the emphasis reversed. By awakening the memory of the tyrannic Duke Frederick—note that as soon as Rosalind's homosexual courtship ends, the force of persecution returns—Jaques de Boys deflates the importance and the effect of the multiple marriages: his "tidings" at first remind us that the separation of a daughter from her father, or of a woman from her beloved, did not initiate the anxiety in *As You Like It*. The usurping Duke Frederick, Jaques de Boys reminds us, remains the real "problem" of the play, and, as a consequence, Rosalind's conclusion becomes, in its effect, impractical: the multiple marriages do not resolve the specific social tensions and oppositions with which the play, or the retreat to Arden, began. We almost feel as if Rosalind's conclusion uses the fantasy structure of wish-fulfillment in dreaming and that Jaques de Boys wakes us from the dream to confront, in the "real" world, the problem that the dreamworks tried, symbolically, to solve.

But, as a countermovement to their sense of awakening, Jaques de Boys's tidings also create a deeper sense of wish-fulfillment and mystery, a sense that inevitably must be attached to, as though caused symbolically by, Rosalind's ceremonial conclusion. Jaques de Boys reports:

> Duke Frederick, hearing how that every day
> Men of great worth resorted to this forest,
> Address'd a mighty power, which were on foot
> In his own conduct, purposely to take
> His brother here, and put him to the sword;
> And to the skirts of this wild wood he came;
> Where, meeting with an old religious man,
> After some question with him, was converted
> Both from his enterprise and from the world,
> His crown bequeathing to his banish'd brother,
> And all their lands restor'd to [them] again
> That were with him exil'd. (V. iv. 154–65)

The effect, which raises real fears of Duke Frederick only to dissolve them immediately without satisfactorily explaining Duke Frederick's conversion, first demonstrates the practical insufficiency of Rosalind's conclusion in isolation, then implies that a magical power does operate in Arden, a power that Rosalind's rituals may have inspired or activated through sympathetic magic. The immediate conjunction of Jaques de Boys's announcement with Rosalind's conclusion, then, makes us feel that contact coordinates the strange events. We feel as if the rituals celebrated by Hymen have extended their powers into other regions—of the forest, or of consciousness—so as to make the conclusion that Rosalind has accomplished occur both as a nuptial and a political fact.

In this sense, then, by its sympathetic association that primarily results from dramatic conjunction with the wedding ceremonies, Jaques de Boys's announcement extends and expands the power that we have attributed to Rosalind's style: because they juxtapose, we attribute the two conclusions to the same cause. The conclusion of *As You Like It* thus ties in the off-stage conversion of Duke Frederick with the predominant second-world strategy of the play: his conversion does not occur because of the vicissitudes of Fortune, but because of the magical effects of Rosalind's style. By translating Nature and Fortune into the voluntary force of style, the conclusion of *As You Like It* places both terms under human control. The Fortune that brings Orlando to Rosalind and that converts Duke Frederick, the sexual nature that draws Phebe to Sylvius, Touchstone to Audrey, and the familial nature that draws Rosalind to her father, reconciles Oliver to his brother, all are subordinated because attributed to the power of Hymen, which appears to be a heavenly intervention but which we know to be a manifestation of Rosalind's style. The conclusion of *As You Like It* dramatizes the determinant effect that style has on both Nature and Fortune, and therefore the conclusion confirms the second-world strategy earlier associated with Duke Senior—the translation of Fortune and Nature into style—as a way to confront and to change, not merely to avoid, the threatening material conditions of the primary world.

"THE LINEAMENTS OF NATURE"

In short, *As You Like It* concludes by elevating art to a position above the antithetic terms Nature and Fortune, by proposing style as the synthesis to the dialectical problem. The play therefore proposes that one solve problems in the material world by transcending them, or by transcending the material world, and translating material conditions into stylistic propositions. *As You Like It* further implies that the only true reconciliations occur not in the world or between the subject and the world but in the mind, purely subjectively. Consequently, to defend against objective opposition, assault from without, one should cultivate one's own subjectivity, should express and discover the self through style, and thereby know the self, achieve self-knowledge. And one could stop there, having identified *As You Like It* with the defense of style and artifice. Yet such a conclusion, one that advocates absorption in style and in self, has no meaning unless placed within a context, a qualification that escapes many critics of *As You Like It*. To conclude from the play that people discover Nature and thus become more fully themselves through art[8] or that the "only real reconciliation between the actual and the ideal . . . is subjective, effected in the mind", (20)[9] one must mistake the part for the whole: *As You Like It* contains and expresses these subjective ideas and ideals, but these ideas do not comprise the play. In fact, the play uses its own expression and dramatization of subjective ideals to explore the practical limitations of subjectivity, to confront subjectivity with real, material conditions.

Part of the difficulty with *As You Like It* arises because the play creates the illusion that the second-world society developed by the protagonists constitutes an entire "world". In *Some Versions of Pastoral*, William Empson gives a hint as to how this illusion comes about: Empson notes that the pastoral form creates or presents two (extreme) worlds to create the illusion that the entire world has been included in the work.[10] In *As You Like It*, the pastoral society itself contains several sets of extremes (the isolated Jaques and the surrounded Duke Senior, the indecorous Touchstone and the fastidious Sylvius, for example), which make us feel, on one level, that the society of the exiled courtiers constitutes a complete world. At the same time, however, the play breaks down this illusion and shows the limitations or boundaries of the second-world society by also including a society of native foresters, "real" shepherds and country people. Although in Shakespeare's source *Rosalynde*, the courtiers who go to the forest identify themselves with the country and, quite unconvincingly, speak of its ways as their own,[11] *As You Like It* enforces a distinction—inevitably a class distinction—between those who come from the court and those who live in Arden. By maintaining a distinction between those who come to and those who live in the forest, *As You Like It* identifies the achievements of the second-world society, the stylistic transcendence of Nature and Fortune, with the particular strategies of one social class.

The encounters between the aristocrats in exile and the natives of Arden, the real shepherds, show us that the ideals of translating Fortune into style or of using art to learn about Nature require for their enactment the privileges, the freedom from material concerns, of the ruling class; or, put another way, the ruling class ideals contradict the material conditions in which other classes live. Rosalind and Celia's entry into Arden and their initial encounter with Corin (II. iv.) nicely demonstrate the native's limited access to the strategy of stylistic abstraction. Touchstone, who serves here as a mediator, making the initial contact with the forest natives, raises the issue of social differentiation and hierarchy in his first words to Corin:

> Touchstone: Holla! you clown!
> Rosalind: Peace, fool, he's not thy kinsman.
> Corin: Who calls?
> Touchstone: Your betters, sir. (II. iv. 66—8)

Corin confirms rather than disputes or ignores Touchstone's observation: "Else are they very wretched," (68). With the social differentiation thus stated, Rosalind inquires of Corin:

> I prithee, shepherd, if that love or gold
> Can in this desert place buy entertainment,
> Bring us where we may rest ourselves and feed.
> Here's a young maid with travel much oppressed,
> And faints for succor. (II. iv. 71—5)

Corin's response to Rosalind's request, as Renato Poggioli has
pointed out, has no counterpart in all of pastoral literature (181).[12]
Corin cannot offer hospitality because he has no title to his land and
flocks, he works as a wage labourer:

> Fair sir, I pity her,
> And wish, for her sake more than for mine own,
> My fortunes were more able to relieve her;
> But I am shepherd to another man,
> And do not shear the fleeces that I graze.
> My master is of chirlish disposition,
> And little reaks to find the way to heaven
> By doing deeds of hospitality.
> Besides, his cote, his flocks, and bounds of feed
> Are now on sale, and at our sheep-cote now
> By reason of his absence there is nothing
> That you will feed on; . . . (II. iv. 75–86)

Rosalind, however, realizes that she and Celia need not depend
solely on the vicissitudes of another's hospitality:

> I pray thee, if it stand with honesty,
> Buy thou the cottage, pasture, and the flock,
> And thou shalt have to pay for it of us.
> Celia: And we will mend thy wages. I like this place,
> And willingly could waste my time in it.
>   (II. iv. 91–5)

I have quoted at some length from this transitional (from
banishment to liberty) scene because I think it important to notice
the particular social relations and exchanges that precede
Rosalind's translation of bad fortune into pastoral style. Here we
can see why it makes no sense to say, as many have, that the forest
"allows" people in general to discover their own Nature: such a
proposition ignores or abstracts from the material conditions that
exist in and that the protagonists bring to the forest. Rosalind and
Celia's gold, or, more precisely, their aristocratic poise that
bespeaks their gold, enables them to translate their fortunes into
the pastoral style of life:

Corin: . . . if you like upon report
              The soil, the profit, and this kind of life,
              I will your very faithful feeder be,
              And buy it with your gold right suddenly.
                                        (II. iv. 97—100)

Corin, however, explicitly points out that he is bound to his
"fortunes" (77) by the material, or economic, circumstances
within which he lives. Only benevolent new masters, by "mend-
ing" Corin's wages, can improve, but hardly translate, *his*
fortunes.

The play establishes here a distinction between what we could
call fixed and variable, or else involuntary and voluntary, fortunes:
Corin's fortunes depend on the actions, dispositions, and dispen-
sations of others, whereas Rosalind and Celia control or translate
their fortunes through and because of their access to gold. The
characters experience this distinction between fixed and variable
fortune as a class distinction in the most basic sense: because of their
access to gold, explicitly *not* because of a "natural" hierarchy,
Rosalind and Celia remain detached from any requirement that
they work. Later in the play Sylvius and Phebe, who seem to live in
the forest but who speak with the courtly rhetoric characteristic of
the pastoral tradition, carry this detachment from labour to an
extreme point. Sylvius, like Rosalind and Celia, has access to
capital—he had planned to buy Corin's master's cottage until
distracted by his love for Phebe—and therefore he can retain a
separation from the explicitly pastoral labours: not only his place
within a literary tradition but also his financial independence
within the play frees Sylvius from physical toil. Although always
referred to as a shepherd or a swain, Sylvius never works at tending
flock; he works only at style, or as Phebe's appointed stylist:

Phebe: But since that thou canst talk of love so well,
         Thy company, which erst was irksome to me,
         I will endure; and I'll employ thee too.
         But do not look for further recompense
         Than thine own gladness that thou art employ'd.
                                        (III. v.   )

Sylvius's detachment from material concerns enables him to

express an ideal attitude toward labour and toward the materials of human subsistence:

> So holy and so perfect is my love,
> And I in such a poverty of grace,
> That I shall think it a most plenteous crop
> To glean the broken ears after the man
> That the main harvest reaps. Loose now and then
> A scatt'red smile, and that I'll live upon. (III. v. 94–104)

For Sylvius, both employment and food remain metaphoric and stylistic, separate and distinct from both actual physical engagement with and the material properties of his environment.

Rosalind and Celia's perception of their environment shows this same sense of detachment from the need for physical labour. As Celia's remark "I like this place, /And willingly could waste my time in it" indicates, they perceive the environment as if it passively contains and nurtures them, allowing them the freedom to use time at will. Corin, however, perceives the environment as an object—"Assuredly the *thing* is to be sold" (II. iv. 96)—and as a place that requires human labour, as a place where sheep graze and are sheared (79). Corin thus takes upon himself the active, nurturing role—"I will your very faithful feeder be"—that Rosalind and Celia had, abstractly and unconsciously, attributed to the environment in general.

Corin, therefore, becomes identified with the materials of his environment, whereas Rosalind and Celia, who own those materials as property, can remain detached from their environment, free to see it subjectively, as an idea, free to translate the environment to suit their internal "nature". Corin's long discussion with Touchstone (III. ii.) displays his nearly tautological relation to Nature as the out-of-doors; Corin and Touchstone differ in that Touchstone can affect Nature with language, can use subjective perception to achieve a different perspective on life:

> In respect that it is solitary, I like it very well; but in respect that it is private, it is a very vild life. Now in respect it is in the fields, it pleaseth me well; but in respect it is not in the court, it is tedious . . . (III. ii. 15–19)

whereas Corin sees Nature as a fixed condition, with laws of cause and effect independent of human will:

> I know the more one sickens the worse at ease he is; and that he that wants money, means, and content is without three good friends; that the property of rain is to wet and fire to burn; that good pasture makes fat sheep; and that a great cause of the night is lack of the sun. . . . (III. ii. 23–8)

As the rest of the discussion makes clear, Corin must understand Nature objectively, as a part of real, material conditions independent of his consciousness, because his life depends upon his own physical relation to Nature. The courtiers use their bodies ceremonially, they kiss one another's hands, and appropriate Nature, "the very uncleanly flux of a cat", (68) as the accoutrements of their style, whereas Corin uses his body to work in and upon Nature: "we are still handling our ewes" (53); "[Our hands] are aften tarr'd over with the surgery of our sheep" (62–63); finally:

> Sir, I am a true laborer: I earn that I eat, get that I wear, owe no man hate, envy no man's happiness, glad of other men's good, content with my harm, and the greatest of my pride is to see my ewes graze and my lambs suck. (III. ii. 73–7)

The events of the play, of course, negate the feeling of independence that Corin's statement implies, which illustrates one of the paradoxes of the "independent" labourer: on one level, Corin's statement correctly asserts that Rosalind, Celia, and Touchstone, who do not earn that they eat, depend for their survival upon others; on another level, the level that the play as a whole explores, those who can depend on the true labour of others rather than on the objective conditions of their environment for their survival attain the *independence* of complete subjectivity, the freedom to change their environment into a "landscape of the mind", a "heart's forest".[13]

By using language to shift his perspective on the forest, Touchstone hints at the subjective independence that the courtiers achieve, but we can see the actual freedom from, or freedom to change, material conditions developed more completely when the aristocrats discuss and use time and space. For example, when Rosalind first meets Orlando in Arden she diverts and charms him by trying to prove the relativity of time:

> Time travels in divers paces with divers persons. I'll tell you who Time ambles withal, who Time trots withal, who Time gallops withal, and who he stands still withal. (III. ii. 308–11)

In response to Orlando's questioning, she then proceeds to tell him with whom Time travels in each of these paces (312–33). In effect, Rosalind proves—declares, actually—that one's subjective feelings, not objective, natural phenomena, determine the "time o'day" (300)—a pleasant conceit, but one that presupposes the capacity to subordinate time to the needs of one's ego. Rosalind's sense of the variability of time, and of the interdependence of time and the emotions, directly contradicts Corin's implicit sense of the fixed nature of time: Corin's sense of being, his sense of *his* subjectivity, derives from his accepting the conditions of Nature as objective realities. Corin's belief "that the property of rain is to wet and fire to burn; that good pasture makes fat sheep; and that a great cause of the night is lack of the sun" (III. ii. 26–8) implicitly opposes Rosalind's subjective attitude toward time in that he keeps natural conditions *disinct* from the emotions. By inference, Corin does not believe, for example, that rain imitates the lover's sorrow, or that the beloved's absense causes the night. Whereas for Rosalind, subjectivity determines the conditions of Nature, for Corin the conditions of Nature determine subjectivity.

The aristocratic protagonists further distort the natural, or in this case really social, conditions of the forest to satisfy their subjective needs, to purge Arden of an alien culture, through their repeated insistence that no people inhabit the forest. We have already seen, for example, that the Duke and his followers call the deer the "native burghers of this desert city", and that Rosalind refers to the forest as "this desert place". Further, Orlando's verse, which Celia reads aloud, proclaims:

> "Why should this [a] desert be?
> For it is unpeopled? No!" (III. ii. 125–6)

And as Jörg Hasler has pointed out in his discussion of dramatic inconsistencies in *As You Like It*, the idea of the desert forest extends beyond mere stylistic conceit and affects the way some of the characters live in Arden: Duke Senior and the courtiers live almost barbarically in caves, although the forest contains enough of a civilization and an economy so that Rosalind and Celia can buy a cottage.[14] The inability to perceive the actual country community, or—expressed another way—the projection of the subjective desire for an unpeopled forest on to the material world, works to determine the conditions of Nature, to control the courtiers' active relation to Nature in the forest. The courtiers purge Arden of people in order to fill the world with their pastoral style.

Here we can see how the generalization that the "forest mirrors one's mind" actually distorts the facts and conditions of the play, restricts the whole play to the privileged perceptions of one class. Only the aristocracy can appropriate the new environment as a subjective entity, an emblem of the mind. This same act of appropriation, while it brings about an accord between mind and Nature for the courtiers, also distorts the objective facts of Nature known and experienced by the country people, for whom the forest merely exists—as the material conditions of time and place, as environment. For Corin, Nature contains and produces the materials with which and conditions in which he works; Audrey, William, and Sir Oliver Martext, the characters most clearly designated as country-dwellers, are the *only* characters in the play who never mention either Nature in general or their environment in particular. The concept of the forest-as-mirror, therefore, attributes a quality to the forest environment, to Nature, that it does not possess: their freedom from labour allows the aristocrats to translate Nature into an aspect of mind, but Nature itself remains objective and other to the minds of the country people. The forest does not mirror William's mind, or Audrey's. The aristocratic protagonists incorporate the forest within their subjectivity, but they can do so only because they remain free from the need to work in the forest, free from the imposed objective conditions of Nature. For Corin, rain helps make good pasture, which makes fat sheep; for the Duke, the climate persuades him who he is.

By translating Nature into an aspect or expression of their own subjective style, the courtiers articulate a harmony between the divergent senses or definitions of *nature*: their intrinsic qualities or fundamental characteristics become identical with the physical world, the out-of-doors; their natures become identical with Nature. But, significantly, the aristocrats must achieve or create this harmony; the harmony does not come about "by nature". As an achieved quality, this harmony between two senses of *nature* also negates Nature in another sense: Nature becomes a phenomenon contrived through human effort, produced through purposive action; Nature becomes its own opposite, culture. The pastoral second-world functions, therefore, to create an environment in which the lineaments of Nature need not have been fixed and determined *a priori*, but in which Nature itself can be culturally determined so as to define the lineaments of a ruling class.

Consequently, the willed misperception of environment in *As You Like It* does not represent mere error, but represents a creative social act, the formation of an ideology. By creating the illusion that the forest mirrors the mind, the ruling class also creates the illusion that Nature certifies all of the social conditions in Arden. The illusion makes us feel that Corin's resignation to and contentment with labour and the ruling class presupposition of freedom from labour both derive from Nature, from an environment that expresses the intrinsic qualities of *all* of its inhabitants. This ideology establishes an ethical application of *nature* in line with two more of Lovejoy and Boas's definitions:

Definition 46. Good "by nature" is that social order in which those having superior "natures" rule: ethical naturalism as the principle of aristocracy.

Definition 48. Good "by nature" is that social order wherein each man exercises only the function for which he is "by nature" adapted. . . .

The extreme flexibility of *nature* in each of these definitions appears in *As You Like It* as a ruling-class identification of consciousness with Nature, which determines the relation of all other classes to Nature. Since the forest mirrors the mind, this ideology implies, the opposition between labour and freedom in Arden does not subject one class to another but helps determine those who have "superior natures" and who "by nature" should rule. Further, the ideology implies, the real shepherd, who does not rule, achieves his own form of superiority, a superiority resulting from his contentment with what he has, a superiority that, as Lawrence Lerner has written in reference to literary shepherds in general, "depends on his staying where he is".[15] The shepherd's labour, presumably, expresses his nature, "the function for which he is 'by nature' adapted", while the freedom and style, the functions for which the aristocracy is "by nature" adapted, express the aristocratic nature. This opposition between labour and freedom, since each activity expresses the Nature of a particular class, appears to constitute a single social order whose qualities are, "by nature", good.

Beneath the romance and the comedy, *As You Like It* articulates an ideological process, whereby the ruling class uses Nature, or its own translation and redefinition of *nature*, to justify its freedom from labour and the subordination of, or struggle against, other social classes. By identifying the class opposition with Nature, and by using Nature to guarantee both its own autonomy and the subservience of others, the ruling class makes it appear as if its second-world strategy has no class contents at all: its ideology creates the feeling that, since each class expresses its own nature through its activity, an "implicitly multi-layered social contract" gets established, the feeling that "class difficulties" have been put "in the context of a view beyond them in the leveling power of nature and imagination". The critic I am quoting here, Harold E. Toliver, comes so close to the truth about *As You Like It*, yet, failing to see the fantasy or ideology that controls this truth, he misses the truth entirely:[16] he does not realize that the ruling class uses Nature and the imagination to separate its freedom from others' labour while transcending all opposition as such between classes. The idea of a "contract" shrewdly implies that all classes have agreed to the separation of freedom from labour for the maintenance of a general social good, identical both with Nature and with the *status quo*. In fact, *As You Like It* establishes no such social contract; its aristocratic protagonists formulate and enact an ideology: they express the particular interests of their own class as if these were identical with universal interests, with the interests of the whole society.

5 *Twelfth Night*

"THE MORALITY OF INDULGENCE"

In 1959 C. L. Barber's book *Shakespeare's Festive Comedy*[1] and John Hollander's article *"Twelfth Night* and the Morality of Indulgence"[2] challenged, with similar arguments, Morris P. Tilley's long-accepted thesis that *Twelfth Night* advocates a mean between extremes. Tilley saw *Twelfth Night* as "a philosophical defense of a moderate indulgence in pleasure, in opposition on the one hand to an extreme hostility to pleasure and on the other hand to an extreme self-indulgence", (pp. 550–1).[3] Hollander reacted against the entire tendency to place *Twelfth Night*, to find a moral "position" for the play. Hollander argued that in *Twelfth Night* Shakespeare substituted "what one might call a moral process for a moral system" (p. 229), that the "essential action" of this moral process is:

> to so surfeit the Appetite upon excess that it "may sicken and so die". It is the Appetite, not the whole Self, however, which is surfeited: the Self will emerge at the conclusion of the action from where it has been hidden. The movement of the play is toward this emergence of humanity from behind a mask of comic type. (p. 230)

This "action", according to Hollander, ensures that Orsino, "embodying the overpowering appetite for romantic love" (p. 231), Olivia, "despite herself, a private glutton" (p. 231), and Sir Toby, with his "huge stomach for food and drink" (p. 237) all "[kill] off" an "excessive appetite through indulgence of it" (p. 238) and supply the "liver, brain, and heart," with "one self king" (I. i. 37–9; pp. 231, 239). Each protagonist surfeits his or her "misdirected voracity" and thereby achieves "rebirth of the unencumbered self", (pp. 238–9). Hollander argued that

97

"everybody" achieves this rebirth: Orsino is supplied with Viola, "his fancy's queen", Olivia with "Cesario or king" (p. 239), "Toby and Maria are married, Aguecheek chastened, etc" (p. 239).

The supposed inclusiveness of Hollander's process—note how his "etc" hedges—depends on his assumption that Feste and Malvolio remain "outside the action" or are "left unaccounted for" (pp. 232, 239), that neither "has doffed his mask of feasting" (p. 233). Hollander asserted that Feste, who "represents" the "very nature" of the action is "unmotivated by any appetite, and is never sated of his fooling" (pp. 232–3), and that Malvolio, who "alone is not possessed of a craving directed outward" is the only character who "cannot morally benefit from a period of self-indulgence" (p. 233).

Barber's argument was a little more abstract, and its thesis, that *Twelfth Night* "moves . . . through release to clarification" (p. 242), depended on the context that his book established. Yet Barber, like Hollander, presupposed that *Twelfth Night* does not demonstrate a static mean between extremes but enacts a movement toward excess that, reaching an extreme point, restores the social order of the play to its healthy norm. Barber's analysis of *Twelfth Night* derives from his assumption that:

> just as a saturnalian reversal of social roles need not threaten the social structure, but can serve instead to consolidate it, so a temporary, playful reversal of sexual roles can renew the meaning of the normal relation. One can add that with sexual or with other relations, it is when the normal is secure that playful aberration is benign. (p. 245)

The "security" out of which the festive release emerges is essential to Barber's analysis of *Twelfth Night*. Barber argued that *Twelfth Night* exhibits "the use and abuse of social liberty" (p. 248); but he qualified "liberty" by a subtle reference to social class: "the play exhibits the liberties which gentlemen take with decorum in the pursuit of pleasure and love" (p. 248).

The word *gentlemen* opens a whole realm of thought that Hollander excludes and that Barber overlooks. By loosely applying the moral process he has abstracted from the play to the play as a whole, instead of to selected characters within the play, Hollander managed to ignore completely the social distinctions that *Twelfth Night* so obviously delineates. He can argue that because Orsino and Olivia have external objects for their appetites, whereas Malvolio loves only himself, Malvolio's indulgence is "perverted" rather than "excessive", (p. 234) and consequently that Malvolio does not deserve "rebirth of the unencumbered self", "fulfillment" in "one self king": "His story effectively and ironically underlines the progress towards this fulfillment in everybody else, and helps to delineate the limitations of the moral domain of the whole play", (p. 235). Hollander gives little attention either to Viola's indulgence or to her fulfillment. He asserts, unconvincingly, that to indulge "she commits" herself to the love-game with Olivia "with redoubled force" (p. 236) and he assumes that to be "Orsino's mistress" will fulfill her "liver, brain, and heart". He supposes that Sebastian has "no real identity apart from Viola" (p. 237). Hollander has little or nothing to say regarding the fulfillment any of the other characters find at the conclusion. In fact, the particular moral process that Hollander has so eloquently described in the abstract does not, when applied to the characters and action of *Twelfth Night*, seem "to encompass everybody" (p. 239): Orsino, Olivia, and perhaps Sir Toby indulge, surfeit, and emerge; but Viola and Sebastian emerge without having indulged, Malvolio indulges and is, according to Hollander, justifiably submerged. The other characters are left out of the process and out of account.

When we apply the abstractions of Hollander's analysis to the characters within the play, we can see that the "morality of indulgence" applies to and protectively circumscribes the ruling class of *Twelfth Night*. According to Hollander, the excessive behavior that is moral when enacted by Orsino, Olivia, and Sir Toby is "perverted" when enacted by Malvolio. In fact, however, Malvolio's self-love differs from the obviously narcissistic pre-occupations of Orsino and Olivia and the egoistic revelry of Sir Toby *only* because decorum forbids one of his rank to "surfeit on himself", (p. 234). Hollander correctly notes that the play does not praise Malvolio "as an example of righteous bourgeois opposition to medieval hierarchies" (p. 234), for Malvolio accepts degree—he opposes only his subordinate position within an hierarchical society. The play, however, does not dramatize strategies of bourgeois opposition so much as of aristocratic protection. Only a privileged social class has access to the morality of indulgence: if the members of the ruling class find their identities through excessive indulgence in appetite, the other characters in the play either work to make indulgence possible for their superiors or else, indulging themselves, sicken and so die.

Barber, like Hollander, deftly sidesteps the issue of social class in his discussion of festive release in *Twelfth Night*, although his descriptions of liberty and festivity seem continually to point toward acknowledgement of social privilege:

> What enables Viola to bring off her role in disguise is her perfect courtesy, . . . Her mastery of courtesy goes with her being the daughter of "that Sebastian of Messalina whom I know you have heard of": gentility shows through her disguise . . . ;
> (p. 248)

or:

> Sir Toby is gentlemanly liberty incarnate, a specialist in it. . . . Because Sir Toby has "faith"—the faith that goes with belonging—he does not need to worry when Maria teases him about confining himself "within the modest limits of order".
> (p. 250)

Barber, however, does not pursue the social aspects of his observations, and the principle of festive release remains, as throughout Barber's book, abstracted from the class relations that constitute its context. Because he abstracts festivity from the class relations in the drama, Barber ignores the effect that social class has on the definitions and applications of such key terms as *courtesy* (in regard to Viola), *liberty* (in regard to Feste), and *decorum* (in regard to Malvolio). For Feste, Barber writes, to "sing and beg"—that is, to work and be dependent—constitutes a "liberty based on accepting disillusion" (p. 253). Barber distinguishes Malvolio's desire "to violate decorum", to rise in stature, from true "liberty" because Malvolio wants to enjoy the authority that accompanies stature, to "relish to the full" the "power" decorum has "over others" (p. 255). The "liberty" of saturnalia, therefore, contrary to Barber's premise, does not reverse social roles, in that the authority relinquished by the ruling class cannot be enjoyed by the subservients because that violation of decorum would contrast with the "genuine, free impulse" (p. 255) with which the ruling class asserts its authority. The violation of decorum must, according to Barber, be treated "as a kind of foreign body to be expelled by laughter" (p. 257).

We cannot really understand festive release or the morality of indulgence until we remove these categories from the realm of abstraction as pure movement or process, place them within social categories, and see that they emerge from the play so as to allow the aristocracy to achieve social consolidation. In other words, we must redefine the moral process as a ruling-class ideology. Each character in *Twelfth Night* embodies a particular individual action—retreat, disguise, aspiration—taken within an hierarchic society. These actions, separate strategies for achieving or asserting identity, when taken together dramatize the social conditions and consequences that circumscribe each individual action. *Twelfth Night*, as a unified action, distinguishes the strategies from one another, the luxury of aristocratic retreat from the catastrophe of a servant's aspirations. Those who talk about movement, process, strategy, sympathy, or essential action outside of the social distinctions that the play maintains censor the ideological aspect of the play. In fact, the social distinctions do not form incidental aspects of a fairy tale romance; they are essential to the plot and theme of *Twelfth Night*. One aristocratic protagonist, after all, becomes a servant, and the difference between her experiences and assumptions as aristocrat and those imposed upon her as servant exposes the problem of social stratification and demonstrates the interdependence of retreat and social station.

"ONE SELF KING" *The Aristocrats*

The second world in *Twelfth Night* does not correspond to a dimension in space; the protagonists retreat inward. While geographically remaining within the primary-world territory, the protagonists retreat from the everyday demands of time, from the restrictions that the primary world imposes on consciousness. The second world in *Twelfth Night* thus appears as less of a physical or spatial fact, more of a private enterprise, an accomplished attitude. In *Twelfth Night* the *self* becomes the second world, as the protagonists replace community with privacy, society with individuality.

In accordance with its emphasis on the privacy of retreat, *Twelfth Night* contains, in fact, three separate retreats from time, three separately created second worlds: Sir Toby's, Olivia's, and Orsino's. Sir Toby, in his retreat, enacts extreme opposition to decorum and to care: "I am sure care's an enemy to life" are nearly his first words (I. iii. 2–3), and he maintains that attitude throughout the play— "I care not; give me faith say I" (I. v. 128–9). Sir Toby's faith obviates the need for him to perform, in the secular sense, works. His faith—that goes with belonging (to Olivia's family and therefore household) as Barber says—obverts care, or social responsibility. Through care one relinquishes privacy, one acknowledges the presence of others in the world. Care, which holds together a community in a system of mutual attention and shared responsibility, is *not* an enemy to life. But Sir Toby's opposition to care in effect isolates him from others, frees him from order ("I'll confine myself no finer than I am", I. iii. 10–11) and from time ("We did keep time, sir, in our catches", II. iii. 93) but also from consequence and from activity:

> Sir Andrew: Shall we [set] about some revels?
> Sir Toby: What shall we do else? were we not born under
> Taurus? (I. iii. 135–8)

Although Sir Toby "belongs" within the social order, he has no permanent, everyday responsibility for the maintenance of that order. Through his freedom from time and responsibility Sir Toby attempts to extend his ego-boundaries so as to convert into a social norm his permanent condition of irresponsibility. Sir Toby, therefore, as part of the narcissitic process that creates the second world, replaces external objects with his own ego, or, inversely, incorporates and consumes all those in his presence: he forces everyone to care for him while using the enforced incompetence of drunkenness and the willed oblivion of time in order to protect himself from the possibility of caring for others. Sir Toby's freedom from time does not, in short, replace permanent everyday responsibility with the temporary holiday celebration of good fellowship; rather, Sir Toby's holiday depends on *his* permanent freedom from responsibility. He uses the mechanisms of revelry and celebration so as to create a private and fundamentally selfish holiday world.

   Olivia retreats from community, from the everyday world, by enforcing a separation between time and society. She imprisons time inside her doors, behind which:

> . . . like a cloistress she will veiled walk,
> And water once a day her chamber round
> With eye-offending brine. (I. i. 27–9)

Olivia makes time meaningless to her life by converting time into pure measurement; she uses time so as to keep her ritual actions— once a day, for seven years—regularly and evenly separated. Olivia's time, therefore, creates stasis and, rather than marking change and transformation, as Feste's song indicates that it does—

> What's to come is till unsure.
> In delay there lies no plenty,
> Then come kiss me sweet and twenty;
> Youth's a stuff will not endure (II. iii. 49–52)

—time for Olivia measures similarity and repetition. Her ritual mourning does not acknowledge death, but, by making the future entirely predictable and controlled, her mourning protects against loss and decay, refuses to mourn. Olivia perverts rather than rejects the communality of care by directing it toward one no longer in the world, reserving care for her "brother's dead love, which she would keep fresh / And lasting in her sad remembrance", (I. i. 30–1). Olivia's private and solipsistic retreat, much more obviously than Sir Toby's, keeps her separate from the needs and desires of others, as her veiled face symbolizes.

   Perhaps, though, regarding Olivia's veil, the emphasis falls on *will* (she *will* veiled walk), on her intentions. Her love for Cesario breaks her out of the privacy of her retreat—she lifts her veil—and returns her abruptly, against her will, to a community, the world of love and of care, which everyday time controls and dominates. A unique stage direction in Shakespeare's works—"*clock strikes*" (III. i. 129)—interrupts Olivia's courtship of Cesario. Hearing the clock, Olivia acknowledges the passage of time and the effect time has on her actions: "The clock upbraids me with the waste of time," (130). When she marries Sebastian, she incorporates a consciousness of time into her pursuit of happiness: "Blame not this haste of mine. If you mean well,/Now go with me, and with this holy man", (IV. iii. 23 – 3). By the end of the drama Olivia's private second world has dissolved into a world of community, the world of time.

Orsino retreats from the community of the everyday world by imposing his will on his environment. He transforms environment into a series of non-autonomous objects and actions, things arranged for his contemplation and commentary. His familiar opening lines clearly indicate this:

> If music be the food of love, play on,
> Give me excess of it; that surfeiting,
> The appetite may sicken, and so die.
> That strain again, it had a dying fall;
> O, it came o'er my ear like the sweet sound
> That breathes upon a bank of violets,
> Stealing and giving odor. Enough, no more,
> 'Tis not so sweet now as it was before. (I. i. 1 – 8)

His own contemplations and comments take precedence over the independent, temporal flow of the music: *Twelfth Night* does not open with music but with a precise, detailed analysis of Orsino's subjective reaction to music, with the projection of Orsino's consciousness. In effect, the Duke converts the objective time that the laws of aesthetic harmony and composition control into the "shapes" of his own "fancy" (14). With the same process of conversion through imposition of will Orsino forces the words and actions of all those in his environment to serve his private, subjective needs. Everything in Orsino's environment—Curio's straightforward language (16), Olivia's straightforward rejection, the "sweet beds of flow'rs" (39), Viola's devout attendance, Feste's "old and antique song" (II. iv. 3)—loses its autonomy and becomes an adjunct of and accompaniment to the Duke's psychological condition, his emotions. Each time the Duke confronts the world he deprives others of their autonomy, superimposes consciousness of his subjective needs on the experiences and needs of others. As a consequence, Orsino attends to his own feelings while he overlooks the feelings others show toward him: Olivia rejects him, Feste mocks him, his page loves him.

Orsino's ability to deprive others of their autonomy converts people into objects and, as a phase within a narcissistic process, it does more: it transforms the objects into aspects of Orsino's subjectivity. By making himself the only subject in the world, Orsino has both withdrawn from and circumscribed the world: he has withdrawn his ego from the world but, by depriving others of their autonomy, he has then drawn the world *into* his ego. The behavior of others in the world thereby appears to be not autonomous action taken by other people but manifestations of Orsino's own subjective feelings. Withdrawing from the world, he has increased his power to control, or to feel in control of, the world.

Each of the three private, inward retreats of *Twelfth Night* extends and expands the potagonist's ego, not by projecting the self into nature but by making the world smaller than, or an aspect of, the self. In each of the second worlds in *Twelfth Night* the protagonist—Sir Toby, Olivia, Orsino—diminishes the time, conditions, and people in the primary world so that the desires and emotions of the self can predominate in, or over, the world. The second worlds of *Twelfth Night*—separate and distinct from one another—each replace the multiplicity of community with "one self king".

"TO HIS IMAGE . . . DID I DEVOTION" *The Ideal Servants*

Viola's entry into Illyria suggests that she, too, will engage in some form of second-world retreat: her personality seems to depend on her ability to master adversity, to control her environment through language, gesture, and disguise. As Barber describes Viola's initial function in the plot:

> The shipwreck is made the occasion for Viola to exhibit an undaunted, aristocratic mastery of adversity—she settles what she will do next almost as though picking out a costume for a masquerade . . . What matters is not the event, but what the language says as gesture, the aristocratic, free-and-easy way she

settles what she will do next and what the captain will do to help her. (pp. 241–2)

Barber, as usual, is more accurate than he realizes: emphasize the word *aristocratic*, and the class aspect of Viola's "mastery" becomes immediately apparent. When she first appears, her relation to her environment parallels that of Orsino to his; she treats the world and the people in it as objects available for her to use. As she "settles" what the captain will do to help her—"I'll serve this duke;/Thou shalt present me as an eunuch to him" (I. ii. 55–6)—she denies, in a subtle way, the captain's autonomy, the possibility of an opposition of wills, the possibility that the captain may be unwilling or unable to help her.

Of course more than just language and gesture allows Viola to decide the "form" of her "intent" (55). She accompanies her calm distribution imperatives by a distribution of money: "For saying so, there's gold" (18); "I prithee (and I'll pay thee bounteously)" (52). In this respect Viola acts much as did Rosalind when entering Arden: she uses the distribution of gold, or of the aristocratic mastery of language that bespeaks gold, to buy the good will of those whom she meets and to purchase stature within a pre-existent, functioning community. Viola, also like Rosalind, has an enthusiastic, playful regard for disguise. She has no particular motive for disguising herself either as a man or as a eunuch, but by adopting disguise she can transform the natural world, whose forces have deprived her of identity and nearly of life, into a playground. Through disguise she plans to transform the objective social conditions that she will find in Illyria into aspects of her consciousness, into subjective qualities, props for the game that she hopes to initiate and control.

In order to control and to treat the environment as an aspect of one's own consciousness, to make of the world a second world, one must maintain sufficient social stature within the primary world. Here we see one of the central distinctions between Rosalind's actions in Arden and Viola's in Illyria: the two protagonists assume different roles in their plays not because of their different temperaments and personalities (Viola's greater deference and timidity, for example), but their personalities appear to differ because of the different social roles that they adopt, or that their disguises force on them. Rosalind, as we have seen, uses her disguise to increase her autonomy; she escapes from the tyrannous persecution by Duke Frederick as she becomes a master, a landowner who hires labour. Viola, however, in adopting her disguise, assumes a subservient position within a functioning society; without at first knowing it, she becomes part of the objectified landscape of Orsino's court. Viola, as a consequence, experiences a gradual and frightening loss of control; her language remains, as Orsino says, "masterly" (II. iv. 22), but never at any subsequent point in the play can she exert the same authority that she did initially over the captain. We can, in fact, chart a course to mark the disintegrating authority and the increasing subservience and dependence that Viola undergoes during the play as we observe her language change from the calm, assured imperatives of the first act:

> Conceal me what I am, and be my aid
> For such disguise as haply shall become
> The form of my intent. I'll serve this duke;
> . . .
> What else may hap, to time I will commit,
> Only shape thou thy silence to my wit, (I. ii. 53−5, 60−1)

to the apostrophes she can utter only in solioquy by Act II:

> Disguise, I see thou art a wickedness
> Wherein the pregnant enemy does much.
> . . .
> O time, thou must untangle this, not I,
> It is too hard a knot for me t'untie, (II. ii. 27−8, 40−1)

to the prayer that, no longer able either to command others or to control her own stage-space, she must utter as an aside:

> Pray God defend me! A little thing would make me tell them how much I lack of a man. (III. iv. 302−3)

Viola's second-world strategy disintegrates as she becomes treated, with increasing humiliation and danger, as an object within the second worlds of Orsino, Olivia, and Sir Toby. Because she disguises herself as a servant, she assumes a "barful" (I. iv. 41) rather than a liberating role; like the other servants in the comedies, Viola—or, Cesario, rather—makes possible the continued liberty of the aristocrats while relinquishing her/his own autonomy.

Whereas Rosalind moves throughout *As You Like It* toward a point of complete, almost mystical control, Viola moves throughout *Twelfth Night* toward a point of complete danger, coincident with her increasing objectification in the role of servant. The final point in Viola's objectification as a servant occurs when Orsino threatens to kill her to "spite" Olivia:

> But this your minion, whom I know you love,
> And whom, by heaven I swear, I tender dearly,
> Him will I tear out of that cruel eye,
> Where he sits crowned in his master's spite.
> Come, boy, with me, my thoughts are ripe in mischief.
> I'll sacrifice the lamb that I do love,
> To spite a raven's heart within a dove. (V. i. 125–31)

Here Viola's initial, partially autonomous, role as mediator between Orsino and Olivia dissolves as Orsino incorporates her within his narcissistic fancy: the value of the servant's life has become incidental to the significance of Orsino's courtship and rejection. What's more, Viola responds to Orsino's whim with total acquiescence; she relinquishes her autonomy by placing her life at the absolute disposal of her master:

> And I most jocund, apt, and willingly,
> To do you rest, a thousand deaths would die. (V. i. 132–3)

Viola, who earlier had shown her aversion from physical combat—"I am one that had rather go with sir priest than sir knight. I care not who knows so much of my mettle" (III. iv. 270–2)—now most willingly participates in violent attack as the object or recipient of the violence. The passive attitude before Orsino's threatened violence that Viola adopts indicates several things about the position and the awareness Viola has achieved by this point in the play. Through her willingness to receive Orsino's violence in contrast with her fear of Sir Andrew's, Viola can of course declare aloud her love for Orsino, both through the sexual implications of "die" and through her adorational response to Olivia's question:

> Where goes Cesario?
>   After him I love
> More than I love these eyes, more than my life,
> More by all mores than e'er I shall love wife. (V. i. 134—5)

But Viola's declaration of love, with the risk the declaration entails for her, raises several obvious problems. For one thing, what can she gain by such a declaration if in fact she is about to be sacrificed, to become an absolute object to be used and discarded by Orsino in his courtship of Olivia? Further, Viola gradually has realized the limitations her disguise and her subservient social role have imposed on her, has seen the authority with which she commanded the sea captain dissolve into her dependence on the good graces of such unreliable intermediaries as Sir Toby and the, to her, bewildering Antonio. Why should she be willing suddenly to give up all her former autonomy, to place herself completely at the mercy of people and forces beyond her control? One possible, but I think only partial, answer to these questions is that Viola knows that she only *appears* to be giving up her autonomy, that she acquiesces only as a rhetorical gesture, as her last act of submission in the role of servant before she has her aristocratic stature, in effect, thrust back upon her. Because she evidently has had a glimpse, through Antonio's mistakings, of the surprise ending of the play—

> Prove true, imagination, O, prove true,
> That I, dear brother, be now ta'en for you!, (III. iv. 375—6)

and:

> He nam'd Sebastian
> . . .
>   O, if it prove,
> Tempests are kind and salt waves fresh in love,
>   (III. iv. 379—84)

—she knows that soon her brother will appear and that she will once again become Viola, an aristocratic woman. Consequently, at last aware that she soon will be freed from disguise, that the liberty of masking has not become a permanent state, hence no longer a liberty, she can transform her dependent condition into a freedom, she can declare as a page some of the amorous and erotic feelings that, as a woman and an aristocrat, it would be indecorous for her to utter.

Carried further, however, Viola's expression of her love for Orsino and of the complete objectification and, ultimately, annihilation that she appears or pretends to be willing to undergo to "do" him "rest" indicates what she and, more important, he assume to be the normative attitude of a servant toward his master. Viola knows that her submission to Orsino declares her love for a social equal, but, significantly, she makes her declaration while posing as a perfect servant, a complete subordinate. Viola's submission to Orsino's mischief is set against not the moral norm that one should not kill one person so as to spite another, but that one aristocrat has no proprietary right over the life of another. Olivia asks "Cesario" to escape Orsino's objectification by announcing "his" newly acquired stature:

> Alas, it is the baseness of thy fear
> That makes thee strangle thy propriety.
> Fear not, Cesario, take thy fortunes up,
> Be that thou know'st thou art, and then thou art
> As great as that thou fear'st. (V. i. 146–50)

The accepted convention seems to be that one escapes from complete, sacrificial subservience only by elevation in stature, by declaring anew or revealing a true identity, not by asserting independence and autonomy from the master.

This brief exchange enacts the aristocratic fantasy of the condition of the ideal servant, as created from within the play by the characters: an aristocrat, albeit with ulterior motives, enacts the servant's willing submission. Viola uses the aristocratic fantasy of what an ideal servant would do for his master and would think of his master so as to demonstrate and declare the love she feels, as a social equal, for Orsino. Viola can use submission to declare her love in part because she knows that her page's disguise no longer imprisons her, but largely because she has never relinquished her class-bound perception of the servant's role and function. Viola fails to realize the vulnerability of the ideal servant: she acts in part

out of the illusion that her perfect service to her master will make
her more desirable, more a subject suitable for his love. She does
not realize that the ideal servant in fact becomes more and more of
an object, part of the environment or landscape, a natural resource
there to be used, less and less of a person with his or her own
autonomous feelings. The strategy of ideal service is the least likely
way for Viola to win Orsino's love; if played out to the full, the
strategy would have forced the master to murder the servant. Only
because Viola can emerge from the assumed role of ideal servant
does she escape the fatal consequences that her submission to
Orsino would have brought down upon her, or, rather, upon
"Cesario".

Antonio's relation to Sebastian parallels Viola/Cesario's to
Orsino. Antonio alone in the play embodies the aristocratic fantasy
of complete devotion to a master. Antonio gives up whatever
stature he may have had—he at one time captained a ship, and, as
Orsino admits, won "fame and honor" doing so (V. i. 59)—in
order to serve Sebastian. Antonio speaks of his relation to Sebastian
as something that has transcended his own will:

I could not stay behind you. My desire
(More sharp than filed steel) did spur me forth, (III. iii. 4—5)

and as adoration, complete subjection before Sebastian's mastery:

If you will not murther me for my love, let me be your servant;
(II. i. 35—6)

. . . to his image, which methought did promise
Most venerable worth, did I devotion; (III. iv. 362—3)

His life I gave him, and did thereto add
My love, without retention or restraint,
All his in dedication. (V. i. 80—2)

Further, Antonio, although aware of Sebastian's stature, loves
Sebastian without hope of financial gain or advancement:

My kind Antonio,
I can no other answer make but thanks,
And thanks; and ever oft good turns
Are shuffled off with such uncurrent pay. (III. iii. 13—16)

In fact, much like the *locus classicus* of the ideal servant, Adam in *As You Like It*, Antonio gives his own money to his master (38–47). Unlike Viola, Antonio senses the ideal servant's vulnerability; his language continually refers to violence, enemies, and danger:

> I have many enemies in Orsino's court,
> Else would I very shortly see you there.
> But come what may, I do adore thee so
> That danger shall seem sport, and I will go; (II. i. 45–8)

> I do not without danger walk these streets. (III. iii. 25)

The danger that Antonio associates with his service to Sebastian, however, comes from outside of the master-servant relationship, from the danger contained within the environment into which his service will lead him.

When Viola, whom he has mistaken for Sebastian, denies him, his sense of the danger implicit in the master-servant relationship suddenly shifts: Antonio comes to feel that the real danger to which he is subject comes from *within* the master-servant relationship. He confides to the two officers—"Let me speak a little. This youth that you see here / I snatch'd one half out of the jaws of death, . . . " (III. iv. 359–60) thereby transforming the representatives of Orsino's authority, his supposed opponents, into his associates, protectors against the satanic evil with which he feels his master now opposes him:

> But O, how vild an idol proves this god!
> Thou hast, Sebastian, done good feature shame.
> In nature there's no blemish but the mind;
> None can be call'd deform'd but the unkind.
> Virtue is beauty, but the beauteous evil
> Are empty trunks o'erflourished by the devil. (III. iv. 365–70)

Antonio later confides similarly to Orsino himself—"A witchcraft drew me hither" (V. i. 76)—completing the shift of his alliance from his own master, his private deity, to the forces of social authority outside the bond of his private, servile adoration.

Antonio, of course, suspects that his master has been incorporated into a position of relative authority within the same social order that he had hoped they would both oppose. This becomes even more apparent when Antonio is brought on stage to see Viola, whom he still takes to be Sebastian, in the company of his enemy, the Duke; as Jörg Hasler has pointed out, Viola's statement of recognition—"Here comes the man, sir, that did rescue me" (V. i. 50)—aggravates Antonio's feeling of rejection rather than creates a feeling of puzzlement, in that Antonio must assume that "rescue" refers to his rescuing Sebastian from the sea, hardly to his intervention in a rather ridiculous street brawl.[4] Consequently, not until Orsino says that Viola has "tended upon" him for three months (99) can Antonio begin to suspect an alternate interpretation of his rejection; only then, for him, does mistaken identity begin to replace the idea of outright rejection. When Sebastian enters, Antonio realizes, of course, that his master has not rejected him, but, as many readers have noted, Antonio, like other outsiders in Shakespeare's comedies, is left out of account in the reunions and reconciliations that the final scene dramatizes. When we think about it, we sense that Sebastian could not conceivably allow his faithful servant to be dragged off to prison by his brother-in-law; Antonio's ending could not possibly be tragic. But the failure of the last scene to emphasize, even to state, Antonio's restored faith in his master's benevolence leaves the dramatic and emotional emphasis that Antonio created stopped at the middle phase—the disillusionment—of his adoration: Antonio's pained recognition of the vulnerability and expendability of the ideal servant sticks with us.

Antonio's recognition of and response to his objectification reverses Viola's. Viola "apt and willingly" allows herself to be treated as the object of Orsino's fancy because she knows that her restored aristocratic stature will also restore her subjectivity, hence her safety. Antonio had imagined for himself a microcosmic safety within the boundaries of his master-servant relationship: as Sebastian's servant he willingly braved the dangers of the world. He found, in the role of servant, a kind of second-world retreat, an imaginary replacement of the primary-world hardships with love and with sport:

But come what may, I do adore thee so
That danger shall seem sport, and I will go. (II. i. 47–8)

He realizes, though, that he cannot achieve freedom or autonomy through ideal service to a master: he has a nearly tragic vision of the potential effects, the possibility of complete objectification, implicit in the role of servant. Subjective fulfillment through ideal service to a master is a fantasy imposed from above; when acted out by the servant, the dangerous consequences of ideal service become manifest. Antonio, like Viola, realizes that creation of a second world requires either an initial or a maintained class status and autonomy. Viola can play out the complete objectification of the ideal servant just before she has her subjectivity restored, when danger has once more become, for her, a sport. Antonio rages against the sudden realization that his subjective love for Sebastian has been objectified, that Sebastian "grew a twenty year removed thing", (89) because, for him, the sport of ideal service has suddenly become a real danger.

"MEANS FOR THIS UNCIVIL RULE" *The Servants*

The ideal service exemplified by Viola and Antonio stands at an extreme within the play; the other servants are more concerned with self and occasionally with material reward for service. The other servants do not retreat into a second world bounded by the master-servant relationship, which, as Antonio and Viola's dangers show, obliterates one's self in pure devotion to a master. Rather, they each engage in service either to achieve some end, such as immediate reward or advancement in station, or else they serve without devotion either to self or other but simply to participate in the primary world of time. In fact, the minor characters, those who perform a specific and limited function in the play, refer explicitly to their consciousness of time. For example, the officer who arrests Antonio becomes impatient with Antonio's outburst against Viola/Sebastian:

What's that to us? The time goes by; away! (III. iv. 364)

Similarly, the priest, called upon to confirm Olivia and Viola/Sebastian's marriage, adds that since the wedding ceremony:

> my watch hath told me, toward my grave
> I have travell'd but two hours. (V. i. 162–3)

By emphasizing their consciousness of primary-world time, Shakespeare makes these functionaries serve the incidental purpose of emphasizing the opposition between their own continued everyday existence and the timeless second worlds that the aristocratic protagonists have created. But another kind of normative service, that in which the servant retains consciousness of his or her own ego needs, more systematically opposes the ideal service of Viola and Antonio.

The most obvious example of this normative service is Feste's, quite obviously service for meed, not for duty. Feste demands and receives material reward from nearly all of the aristocrats in the play: Sir Toby and Sir Andrew (II. iii. 31–4), Orsino (II. iv. 67–9; V. i. 27–49), Viola (III. i. 43–53), and Sebastian (IV. i. 19). Only Olivia is omitted, and I think that we must assume, despite Feste's claim to have his own house (III. i. 5–7), that Feste is a regular dependent in Olivia's household: at least Maria's warning to Feste about Olivia's anger at his absence (I. v. 1–30) and Viola's association of Feste with "the Lady Olivia's father" (II. iv. 11–12), as well as Feste's oblique admission that he "belongs" to Olivia (V. i. 8–9) suggest such a dependence. Feste's nearly obsessive concern with payment for services forms an obvious and absolute contrast with Viola's attitude toward material compensation; when Olivia offers to pay Viola for delivering Orsino's message, Viola responds abruptly:

> I am no fee'd post, lady; keep your purse;
> My master, not myself, lacks recompense. (I. v. 284–5)

Olivia's reaction, in effect, inverts Viola's disregard for material reward and her subordination of herself within the boundaries of the ideal master-servant relationship; Olivia recognizes an essentially aristocratic quality in Viola's contempt for material payment. After Viola departs, Olivia recalls in soliloquy her asking Viola about her parentage. Something that occurred between the original question (277–9) and Viola's departure (288)—it can only be Viola's refusal of payment—has confirmed for Olivia the truth of Viola's response:

Olivia: "What is your parentage?"
"Above my fortunes, yet my state is well:
I am a gentleman." I'll be sworn thou art.
(I. v. 289—91)

In fact, Viola's faith in the immutability of her class status and her residual belief that she can remain above material concerns allow her to adopt the aristocratic attitude toward service and toward payment; Olivia recognizes that only an aristocratic personality could formulate an attitude of such subservience, and she responds to the aristocratic foundation of Viola's personality rather than to the subservient actions by which Viola's true class status, paradoxically, manifests itself.

Feste's dependence on material payment corresponds to his total indifference to the source of the payment. Feste roams from Olivia's household to Orsino's and shows no allegiance to any one master that could not, apparently, be bought by another, as, for example, Orsino pays Feste to defy Olivia's commands and bring Olivia out to speak with him (V. i. 41—4). Because Feste performs for an audience as a professional, he does not depend on the master-servant bondage; as many have noted, and as Feste's concluding song emphasizes, his role within the play recalls Shakespeare's role *vis-à-vis* the audience. But we should not make too much of Feste's independence. Although free of a patron, he depends on patronage, and he has hardly achieved anything like the independence of the journeyman wage labourer. In fact, rather than indicating the modern or bourgeois spirit, Feste's independence, his desire for continued material reward, for the purchase of his services, merely shows the other side of his faith both in the rigid social hierarchy and in his fixed place within the social system. His service occurs without flattery and hence without aspiration: although independent of a particular master, Feste cannot imagine himself as independent of his social role as fool, jester, clown, or buffoon. Feste exhibits self-effacement rather than personal vanity, *except* in so far as he identifies his self with his social role; he quickly comes to the defense of fools (I. v. 97—8), and his grudge against Malvolio develops largely because of Malvolio's attack on the institution of "these set kind of fools" (83—9; cf. V. i. 370—7).

Feste's version of independence, therefore, differs from bourgeois independence such as Shylock's, in which one's stature depends only on one's wealth, as well as from what might be called renaissance independence in which, as Enid Welsford has written, "self-expression rather than fulfillment of vocation" was the "proper aim for the individual".[5] Feste expresses his independence as the complete negation of self within the vocation, the social position; Feste is enclosed within the medieval hierarchies as much as Sir Toby, who, according to Barber, "lives at his ease, enjoying heritage, the something-for-nothing which this play celebrates" (p. 250). Feste's attitude and Sir Toby's differ only in that Sir Toby's vocation—"gentlemanly liberty incarnate"—guarantees him something for nothing, allows and encourages his absorption in self, whereas Feste's vocation guarantees nothing and requires his continued subordination of self to the needs and whims of others.

The other servants in the play—Maria, Valentine, and Curio (I do not quite know how or where to place Fabian)—also subordinate themselves to the needs of their social superiors, but through flattery and imitation rather than, as with Feste, through diversion. In the first scene of the play Valentine and Curio exist primarily in order to give the very echo to Orsino's extravagant use of language. Curio supplies the vehicle—

> Will you go hunt, my lord?
> >What, Curio?
> >>The hart.
> Why, so I do, the noblest that I have (I. i. 16–17)

—that Orsino's poetic license operates; Valentine outdoes Orsino in his complex application of metaphoric language:

> . . . like a cloistress she will veiled walk,
> And water once a day her chamber round
> With eye-offending brine; all this to season
> A brother's dead love, which she would keep fresh
> And lasting in her sad remembrance. (I. i. 27–31)

Valentine and Curio, like Duke Senior's counters in *As You Like It*, perform the function expected of subordinates in the second world by assuring the aristocratic protagonist that his version of retreat is not a solitary madness but is a way of reorganizing life and thereby transforming society. They extend Orsino's private second-world retreat out into his environment; by imitating Orsino they dissolve his sense of a boundary between his narcissistic withdrawal and the resistance of the outside world.

Maria has a function similar to Valentine's and Curio's, although she has a more complex dramatic role in that she helps maintain the second-world retreats of two distinct, and in some ways opposed, social superiors: she helps to maintain the quiet and decorum of Olivia's house of mourning while encouraging Sir Toby in his continuous revelry. As the prime mover in the plot against Malvolio—she writes the letter, plants the bait, places the witnesses, prepares Olivia, goads Malvolio, even thinks up Feste's guise as Sir Topas—Maria alone gives shape and direction to Sir Toby's indulgence, which, as Fabian reports at the conclusion, has won her Sir Toby himself:

> Maria writ
> The letter at Sir Toby's great importance,
> In recompense whereof he hath married her. (V. i. 362—4)

Significantly, despite her continuous encouragement of Sir Toby's revelry, she never, as it were, burns her bridges; not until Malvolio reveals the material evidence of the forged letter does Olivia have any suspicion that Maria has been working at cross-purposes, to dissolve as well as to maintain the ritual decorum of the household. For Maria has been serving Olivia's interests as well as Sir Toby's: Maria warns Sir Toby—twice (I. iii. 4—6; II. iii. 72—4)—and Feste (I. v. 1—4) about offending Olivia. Perhaps aware of the importance Malvolio holds for Olivia (e.g. III. iv. 62—3), Maria makes sure that word of her collaboration with Sir Toby does not get back to her mistress. Despite her ambitious role in the plot against Malvolio, Maria never challenges Malvolio to his face, although frequently she taunts him while he is leaving (II. iii. 125) or after he has left the stage. Against Maria's involvement in the Malvolio-plot balances her serious concern for the maintenance of order—not, as may be the case with Malvolio, because of any personal predilection for decorum, but because her mistress wants the house to remain sad and civil. Because Maria does not care about the principle of decorum, she only wants Sir Toby to "confine" himself (I. iii. 8—9) and Feste to excuse his transgressions "wisely" (I. v. 30); she worries that the revelry she encourages might interfere with the illusion of decorum that she helps Olivia maintain. As a result, Maria encourages a particular *kind* of revelry: she transforms Sir Toby's drunken carousals and midnight catches into a sport that requires silent observation and, for the most part, non-interference. She manages to confine Sir Toby, to bring about the peace and quiet that she several times implores (e.g. II. iii. 85, 103; III. iv. 134) by diverting him to a game that must be played, as Fabian says, with "peace, peace, peace" (II. v. 51, 57), "no way but gentleness, gently, gently" (III. iv. 110).

Maria facilitates both Sir Toby's and Olivia's second-world retreats, and in such a way as to encourage the coexistence of the two, despite their opposite natures. She supplies the echo to both of her masters, and assures both that others share their self-indulgent, timeless vision of the world, that the second world extends beyond the boundaries of their own egos. Her performance of this function, however, differs from Viola's and Antonio's ideal service and from Feste's professional service: she does not obliterate her own ego within her vocation or her servile capacity; rather, she uses service as a means of aspiration, for transcendence of service. Her service to Sir Toby proves the point, in that Sir Toby marries her with no other dowry but the jest against Malvolio (cf. II. v. 182–5). Her service to Olivia may also be a strategy for social aspiration, which the undercurrent of competition for favour among all of the servants in *Twelfth Night* suggests exists within each household. We see elements of this competitive aspiration among servants, for example, when Valentine discusses Orsino's attitude toward Viola/Cesario:

> If the Duke continue these favors towards you, Cesario, you are like to be much advanc'd; he hath known you but three days, and already you are no stranger.
>
> Viola: You either fear his humor or my negligence, that you call in question the continuance of his love. (I. iv. 1–6)

Valentine expresses, clearly if subtly, the awareness of stature, the importance of remaining in favour, and the uncertainty introduced to the household by the arrival of a new servant.[6] Viola's statement seems to respond to some threatening or foreboding element contained within the tone of Valentine's seemingly off-handed statement; or else, perhaps, Viola herself introduces the topic of inconstancy, indicating the natural concern a new servant would have with the constancy of the master's favours. Maria may well know of a similar potential inconstancy in Olivia's favours; in fact, Malvolio warns·her of such:

> Mistress Mary, if you priz'd my lady's favor at any thing more than contempt, you would not give means for this uncivil rule. She shall know of it, by this hand. (II. iii. 121−4)

This acknowledgement of inconstant favour, and Malvolio's scolding and threatened report, combine to motivate Maria's action against Malvolio: her plot, among other things, humiliates a favoured fellow-servant.

Throughout *Twelfth Night* aspiration inevitably involves displacement. Viola's sudden rise to favour has displaced Valentine and Curio, both in that she assumes Valentine's function as Orsino's ambassador and in that Orsino literally removes Valentine and Curio from his environment to place Viola there alone:

> Orsino: Who saw Cesario, ho?
> Viola: On your attendance, my lord, here.
> Orsino: Stand you awhile aloof. Cesario,
>   Thou know'st no less but all; (I. iv. 10−13)
>
> Orsino: Let all the rest give place. [*Curio and Attendants retire.*]
>   Once more, Cesario . . . (II. iv. 79)

Viola accomplishes this displacement involuntarily: her aristocratic nature draws her to the Duke's aristocratic bias. Because of her innate gentility, her imitation and extension of Orsino's language and mood is natural rather than acquired; she achieves her privileged position within Orsino's household because he recognizes elements of himself in Viola: "thou dost speak masterly" (II. iv. 22), that is, like a master, he remarks. Maria, too, imitates her mistress, right down to their handwriting, which no one—but Olivia herself (V. i. 345−7)—can tell apart. She achieves the temporary displacement of her rival Malvolio by encouraging him to imitate a false Olivia, the love-sick Olivia created by the forged letter. By the time Malvolio is restored to his place in Olivia's favour, Maria has been freed from the consequences of duplicity toward her mistress, having married into Olivia's family.

The sense of aspiration, either to greater favour or to a higher rank, manifested by Valentine and by Maria, contradicts Feste's medieval immersion in his vocation. Maria, especially, suggests the rudiments of the bourgeois belief in reward for individual merit and accomplishment. Through her service to Sir Toby she transcends service, rises to a higher social position. Her vocation allows her to express and to fulfill herself; this sense of self as an entity apart from service and apart from the bondage of service to one particular master suggests the initial phase of the development of the bourgeois consciousness, of the ideology of individual reward and opportunity. Maria is hardly a proto-bourgeoise, in that her aspiration supports and confirms rather than challenges the continued validity of aristocratic privilege, but with her abilities to separate self from vocation, to express self apart from imposed duty, and to earn by her actions advancement in social degree, only Maria in *Twelfth Night* indicates the bourgeois and Puritan emphasis on independence, competition, and the association of stature with merit.[7]

"TO BE COUNT MALVOLIO"

My use of the word *only* in the preceding sentence must have brought many readers up short. Surely, according to most readers of *Twelfth Night* Malvolio represents the spirit of bourgeois independence. Although few would argue that through Malvolio Shakespeare satirically portrays a Puritan, most accept that Malvolio embodies the modern emphasis on economy, that, as Oscar James Campbell has written, Malvolio is "an enemy to the time-honored English hospitality and liberality because of the strain it puts upon his lady's purse".[8] To an extent, Malvolio seems a representative "modern", partially because he resists the traditional hospitality of the English great house that supports such aristocratic ne'er-do-wells as Sir Toby and Sir Andrew, more so because, in direct contrast with Feste, Malvolio finds his vocation to be a humiliation and, he hopes, a temporary restriction. "Art any more than a steward?" (II. iii. 114), Sir Toby taunts him; and I suppose that Malvolio probably thinks to himself—"Yes; I am Malvolio". His sense that he is not bound to his vocation or to his degree, but that he has some form of personal autonomy that can be recognized and rewarded by society anticipates the modern separation of self from vocation.

But Malvolio expresses aspiration quite differently from Maria. Maria works so as to maintain the two second-world environments, the willed freedoms from time, established separately by Sir Toby and by Olivia. Maria's aspiration grows out of and depends upon the quality of the work that she performs; she rises in class as a reward for her service. Malvolio's aspiration—"To be Count Malvolio!" (II. v. 35)—does not depend on the work that he performs; he thinks of aspiration as a sudden elevation, a jump in class status that will occur because of the intervention of fortune (23) or of "Jove and my stars", (172). Malvolio, that is, has the fantasy that he will jump class not as a result of the actions within the everyday world of time that he is ordered to perform but through the transformation of the everyday world into a world of wish-fulfillment, of projected desire. The yellow stockings that he is asked to wear will not, he feels, win Olivia; they will merely seal the contract that Fortune has drawn up. His sense of aspiration, and concomitantly of his own self-worth, is a second-world fantasy, an attempt to transform the world of time and space into a leisured world structured around a personal whim, to replace environment with ego. In this regard, Malvolio's absolutely opposes the ideal service embodied by Viola and Antonio: the ideal servant is vulnerable because treated like an object by the master; the aspiring servant—what might be called the subjective or the self-conscious servant—is vulnerable because he adopts aristocratic methods, the aristocratic attitude toward the material world, without the implicit protection from the hardships of the world guaranteed by aristocratic status.

Ultimately, there is no fundamental difference between Malvolio's fantasy of narcissistic withdrawal into a world in which he can be Count Malvolio, sitting in state, "having come from a day-bed" (45, 48) and Orsino's narcisstic withdrawal into the Petrarchan conventions and the beds of flowers. The two second-world fantasies differ only in the social reaction and response that they elicit. Those near Orsino confirm his withdrawal from time: they echo his language and thereby subordinate the world and their autonomy in the world to the Duke's ego, they assure Orsino that he is neither solitary nor mad. The social reaction to Malvolio's second world is just the opposite: others cut Malvolio off from the world, imprison him in darkness; they disconfirm his sense perceptions and accuse him of being mad. Certainly, madness pervades the play, but whereas Sir Toby and Orsino use madness as an indulgence, and Sebastian and Olivia find their wishes fulfilled in their madness, only Malvolio confronts madness as a restriction and a limitation.

Malvolio's imprisonment marks the limit that class status imposes on the "morality of indulgence". The fantasy that leads to Malvolio's imprisonment—his love for Olivia and his vision of himself as a Count—is not in the abstract ridiculous or perverse. Only when we apply the ruling-class assumptions about degree and decorum does it seem that Malvolio is sick of self-love, whereas Orsino and Olivia seem to engage in healthy, therapeutic folly and deceit. Nothing in the play supports Hollander's statement that Malvolio "alone is not possessed of a craving directed outward, towards some object on which it can surfeit and die; he alone cannot morally benefit from a period of self-indulgence", (op. cit. p. 233). Such a statement merely represents the critic's wholehearted adoption of the aristocratic attitude toward an indulgence manifested by someone of inferior stature. Orsino, Olivia, and Sir Toby behave just as egocentrically as does Malvolio, and Malvolio, like them, directs his indulgence outward in order to gratify his ego and to expand his ego-centered world. But, Hollander argues, aristocratic indulgence is moral or, as others have said, an "education in matters of love",[9] whereas Malvolio's indulgence is perverse (Hollander), a parody (Jenkins), an extreme (Phialas), a violation of decorum and of the social order (Barber).

A ruling-class ideology operates within the play and prevents Malvolio from creating his own antithetic second world. The second world that Malvolio tries to create, however, is not antithetic to that ideology, for Malvolio accepts and supports the aristocratic assumptions about the need for respect, decorum, and propriety. The charge against Sir Toby—"Is there no respect of place, persons, nor time in you?" (II. iii. 91−2) − is retained, emphatically, in Malvolio's fantasy: "telling them I know my place as I would they should do theirs" (II. v. 53−4). It is quite wrong to see Malvolio's fantasy as egalitarian or as a bourgeois opposition to aristocratic norms. Malvolio attends scrupulously to each aspect of aristocratic behavior, and in fact part of what he would hope to accomplish as Count Malvolio would be the "amendment" of Sir Toby's behavior, the restoration of Olivia's family to normality and decorum. Barber wrongly says that Malvolio has a "secret wish . . . to violate decorum himself" (p. 255). Rather, hoping to achieve the stature into which he was not born, Malvolio (perhaps, surprisingly, like Othello) profoundly respects the superficial accoutrements of rank, the display of decorum. Before he discovers Maria's forged letter Malvolio violates decorum only in that, while still a steward, he indulges aloud in his fantasies of aspiration. The enactment of fantasy must remain the aristocratic prerogative.

There is nothing tragic about Malvolio. The way his aspiration develops and is placed within the drama makes him, in fact, comic in the most elementary—the Bergsonian—sense of the word: he is a complex, dignified man who suddenly is reduced to a mechanism, an object. This reduction occurs when and because his private, second-world fantasy is drawn from him, brought from the world of ideas and mental abstractions out into the material world of time, actions, and community. The letter that Malvolio stoops to pick up marks, from his point of view, the boundary between these two worlds; his private (if overheard) fantasies take on objective status in the forged letter. The letter seems to Malvolio a license for an exclusively aristocratic privilege: to transform a private, narcissistic fantasy into public behavior. His narcissism does become public, enacted in the world, but the letter actually binds rather than licenses him: the letter prescribes Malvolio's actions to a set of imposed restrictions, rather than permits his behavior to be, in true second-world fashion, modulated only by his changeable, subjective humour. The restrictions—the cross-garters, the enforced smiling, which so obviously go *against* his humour ("Sad, lady? I could be sad. This does make some obstruction in the blood, this cross-gartering, but what of that?" III. iv. 20–2)—make him comic, largely because at the very moment at which he feels that he is at last enacting his subjective fantasies, we are aware that, more than ever, he is being manipulated, treated like an object.

When being treated like an object, Malvolio is in effect restored to his place within the social hierarchy. Malvolio's reduction moves in the exact opposite way from Viola's restoration of stature and thereby of autonomy. Viola helps to maintain and to confirm the whims and fantasies of her master, and she does so in part as a mediated expression of her love for him. Malvolio enacts his own fantasies, as an *immediate* expression of his love for Olivia. Temporarily, Viola's willed subordination and Malvolio's willed aspiration have the same effect: both Viola and Malvolio become objectified, imprisoned within the role of servant. When her aristocratic identity is discovered or revealed, however, Viola's objectification reverses, and Orsino acknowledges her as an equal, her "master's mistress" (V. i. 326); Viola becomes a subjective participant in the social ceremonies of and beyond the conclusion. Malvolio, however, has his sanity discovered or revealed only to be confirmed as an object of laughter—"the most notorious geck and gull /That e'er invention play'd on" (343–4)—and, for Feste, of revenge (376–7). The conclusion of *Twelfth Night* contains an element of the Patient Griselda myth—complete subservience leads to unexpected elevation—as qualified by the aristocratic face behind Viola's subordinate mask; essentially, however, the conclusion confirms the aristocratic fantasy (Maria is, discreetly, kept off-stage) that clarification is achieved when people are released from indulgence and restored to the degree of greatness with which they were born.

"ALL IS FORTUNE" *Ideology*

Twelfth Night develops a fundamental distinction between Malvolio's trust in fortune and Viola's. Both characters, pretty clearly, attribute their success or their chances for success in love to a force outside of their own motives and actions. Viola calls this external, controlling force "time", but she imagines the abstraction as something personal, to which or to whom she can speak and commit herself:

> What else may hap, to time I will commit; (I. ii. 60)

> O time, thou must untangle this, not I,
> It is too hard a knot for me t' untie. (II. ii. 40–1)

Malvolio speaks more explicitly theistically in his references and addresses to the external force to which he commits himself. He assigns all power over earthly success or failure to "fortune":

'Tis but fortune, all is fortune; (II. v. 23)

Saying, "Cousin Toby, my fortunes, having cast me on your niece"; (69–70)

but he associates the relatively abstract force of fortune with quasi-religious mechanisms:

I thank my stars, I am happy. . . . Jove and my stars be praised!
(170–2)

I have lim'd her, but it is Jove's doing, and Jove make me thankful! . . .
. . . Well, Jove, not I, is the doer of this, and he is to be thank'd.
(III. iv. 74–83)

Among recent critics of *Twelfth Night* there has been more discussion, disagreement, and confusion about the issue of time and fortune and their different effects on Viola and Malvolio than about any other issue in the play. I think that some of the confusion, at least, derives from Julain Markels's article "Shakespeare's Confluence of Tragedy and Comedy: *Twelfth Night* and *King Lear*".[10] Markels set up an opposition between fortune and custom, and he argued that the theme of both *Twelfth Night* and *King Lear* is that "man must stand fast by custom even in the face of Fortune" (p. 88), that the "central villainy" in both plays is the belief in "capricious fortune" instead of "stable customs" (p. 81). In order to get to this thesis about villainy and fortune, Markels asserted that Malvolio, like Oswald, Goneril, and Edmund, has faith in "the rule of capricious fortune instead of stable customs with cosmic sanctions" (p. 81), and, further, that Shakespeare everywhere opposes fortune to degree, that when degree is left out of the social order, "fortune's devotees" (e.g. Richard III, Edmund) can "get in the door" (p. 81).

In fact, however, neither in *Twelfth Night* nor anywhere else does Shakespeare oppose fortune itself to degree or custom. *As You Like It*, as we have seen, initially opposes Fortune to Nature, and the ruling-class ideology within the play works to reconcile and identify the opposing terms so that the extant class structure can appear to be determined and justified by Nature. *Twelfth Night*, however, opposes fortune (as in chance) to human action and accomplishments, and the ruling-class ideology, which Malvolio *supports*, works to keep these opposing terms separated and distinct. By attributing degree and custom, the determinants of class status, to fortune rather than to action, the ideology fixes the social structure: it encourages a passive acceptance of one's social station and attributes the possibility for a rise in station to a force beyond human motive and control.

Some critics realize Markels's error and acknowledge that belief in fortune supports the customary social hierarchy; because most of these critics believe that Malvolio tries to upset the customary social hierarchy, however, each argues that Malvolio either does not believe in fortune or that he does so in the "wrong" way. Carl Dennis,[11] for example, argues—Malvolio's protestations notwithstanding—that, in contrast with Viola and Sebastian who "regard fate as a power outside their control" (p. 70), Malvolio believes that merit, not fortune, causes his ascension (p. 72). B. S. Field, Jr,[12] argues that Malvolio submits himself to fortune in the wrong way: whereas Viola submits to fortune and "makes no attempt to alter that which is inalterable" (p. 194) and Sebastian has the " 'right' attitude toward the gifts and blows of Fortune" in that he does not consider whether or not he deserves what he has received (p. 196), Malvolio assumes that fate is on his side, and therefore he misses the essential point of Viola's and Sebastian's stoicism—he thinks he *deserves* the advantages of fortune (pp. 198–9). Yet Field's assumption that Malvolio believes in his deserts any more than do Viola and Sebastian is pure assertion, based on a backward interpretation of the play and on some tortured syllogisms: because stoicism is good and in *Twelfth Night* all good characters are rewarded, Malvolio, who is not rewarded, is not stoical. Free Field's analysis from his assumption that the conclusion marks a fair distribution of reward and punishment, and it will become clear that Malvolio's actions do not, after all, differ greatly from Viola's; he is more active and more optimistic in pursuit of his fate because he has been given good reason to be so, not because he has the "wrong" attitude toward fortune.

Viola's, and Sebastian's, faith in fortune is not misplaced, for fortune, more than human action, dominates the conclusion. It is perchance that Viola herself was saved (I. ii. 6) and it is more than chance—more like destiny—that she and Sebastian are reunited and that she becomes Orsino's mistress. But the conclusion not only enforces the benevolence of fortune, it also emphasizes the restrictions on that benevolence: the conclusion applies fortune as a class-bound concept. Rather than seek fine discriminations between Malvolio's trust in fortune and Viola's, we should note that fortune rewards Viola for her faith and punishes Malvolio for his. In fact, the play concludes not with a sense of harmony and inclusion—the inclusion comprises only the two, perhaps the three, aristocratic couples—but of opposition, with, as Alexander Leggatt notes, the happiness of the lovers and the "miracle" of Cesario alternating with the "battered condition" of the clowns and "played off against the uncontrollable world of time".[13] Leggatt notices everything about this opposition but its class contents: the rewards of fortune, and of freedom from time, are circumscribed by the ruling class, but fortune is *separated* from Malvolio. Contrary to everything Markels's article asserted about it, fortune in *Twelfth Night* restores degree and decorum to the world of the play.

Several critics have tried to purge fortune of the class-bound qualities that the conclusion enforces. L. G. Salingar,[14] for example, believes that the second half of *Twelfth Night* "stresses the benevolent irony of fate" (p. 128). Aware, perhaps, that this irony is benevolent only for some of the characters, that it is malevolent for or indifferent to others, Salingar relies on the familiar critical abstractions—balance and complement—so as to keep the "design" of the play intact and free of all class-conflict and ideology: Antonio, according to Salingar, is "outside the main sphere of the comedy" (p. 131), he "helps keep the comic balance" (p. 132); the Malvolio sub-plot is "complementary to the problem of 'time' in the main plot" (p. 133). More recently, F. B. Tromly[15] has argued that *Twelfth Night* shows that "one can come to terms with life only by accepting the nature of things—delusion, vulnerability, and mortality" (p. 59). Orsino, Olivia, Viola, and Sebastian do so, he says, and therefore nature draws them to happiness (p. 68) whereas Malvolio is excluded from happiness because of his "secret desire . . . to violate the social order" (p. 66).

Salingar and Tromly probably consider their interpretations of *Twelfth Night* to be "neutral"; they certainly acknowledge no ideological basis for their generalizations about benevolence and happiness. But the ideological implications of what they say about *Twelfth Night* are grossly apparent. Fate, or the nature of things, they suggest, is a force outside of and beyond human control; one should respond to fate with passive acceptance. Further, happiness and benevolence consist of a restored social order, which excludes all those who seek to violate decorum (that is, to rise in class), or else of a "triumph of natural love" (Salingar, op. cit. p. 122) for the ruling class, which balances against the defeat and exclusion of those "outside the main sphere of the comedy"—that is, in the sub-plot; that is, the servants and subservients. In short, some obvious social implications must accompany the advice to accept fortune, the benevolent irony of fate, or the nature of things; *Twelfth Night* shows that the ruling class benefits by such counsel and that others do not. The ideology is included as a theme *within* the play. *Twelfth Night* does not encourage its audience to accept the vicissitudes of fortune stoically; rather, the play shows that such moral advice serves the interests and fills the needs of a particular social class. Critics who abstract the aristocratic attitude toward fortune from the class contents of *Twelfth Night* and designate the aristocratic attitude as the theme of the whole play avoid recognizing an ideology within *Twelfth Night* by adopting the ruling-class ideology as their own.

Which is exactly what Malvolio does *in* the play: he actually threatens the social order much less than he seems to. Just as he has the greatest respect for all of the accoutrements of aristocratic rank, just as he imitates the aristocracy in attempting to devise a second-world fantasy, he also adopts the ruling-class ideology in attributing his success, or his chances for success, to fortune, to Jove and his stars. Joan Hartwig[16] has noted that Malvolio wants to attribute the control of events to Jove because "as long as events are in the hands of a non-human control, man cannot destroy or divert the predetermined order" (p. 506). Hartwig observes that Sebastian is "manipulated by Fate or by Fortune; Malvolio, by Maria and Feste" (p. 510), but she reduces the importance of her observation by concluding only that "human manipulators parody supra-human control" (p. 510). Yet much more than parody operates here. Maria and Feste, acting upon Malvolio, represent the antithesis of chance—human will. By manipulating Malvolio, creating his destiny, they demonstrate the implicit limitation of the ruling-class attitude that "all is fortune".

"All is fortune" implies that people relate to nature as passive recipients who accept the "nature of things", that fortune, primarily but not exclusively through birth, will determine one's place in the social hierarchy. The fantasy assumes that fortune certifies nature, that ultimately fortune and nature are identical. By accepting this fantasy, Malvolio refuses to act except when instructed from above, by what he assumes to be his "stars", and he thus becomes vulnerable to the actions of those who do act within nature. Just as Malvolio cannot see the manipulations of Maria and, later, Feste, the ruling-class ideology that "all is fortune", that fortune creates and determines nature, is meant to keep people, especially servants, blind to the opposite proposition: that people create nature as they act within time, as they bring about changes in the social order. The ruling-class ideology in *Twelfth Night* unifies the several aristocratic separate and private retreats into a single second-world strategy; the assertion that "all is fortune" and that one should submit to the nature of things attempts to fashion an escape from the responsibilities of the world of time. In *Twelfth Night* Shakespeare acknowledges the existence of the impulse toward retreat from time and from nature, but he does not make the impulse a universal "theme"; rather, he identifies the impulse with the class interests that it serves and he sets the attempt to equate nature with fortune against the everyday world in which people create their own nature and their own fortune, the world of history.

6 *Henry IV, Part One*

"IF I DO GROW GREAT, I'LL GROW LESS" *Falstaff*

Henry IV, Part One, like the comedies with which I have grouped it in this study, contains two clearly demarcated worlds, which we can follow tradition and call the worlds of the tavern and of the court. In this particular play, however, the process I have been consistently trying to identify and explain, the process by which the second world *functions* for the protagonist as part of a strategy for living with maintained or increased stature in the primary world, emerges into the open. Despite the enormous critical disagreements as to precisely what Hal does in the play, as to precisely what benefit he derives from his habitation in Eastcheap, critics do agree that Hal uses the tavern to work his advantage. Hal says so himself: in his famous soliloquy, about which more later, he declares that the tavern world only seems a world of holiday leisure, that in fact the tavern constitutes for the Prince himself a world of "everyday" work, the work of fabricating a public image that will consolidate his eventual political control of the kingdom. In short, in *1 Henry IV* we must perceive, because the protagonist himself perceives, that the distinction between first and second world dissolves when taken beyond a certain point; in the second world of Eastcheap, as in Arden, Belmont, and elsewhere, the protagonists do not enter and discover an autonomous world of play, ritual, and timelessness, but they assert in a new location their own freedom from work, law, and time—*their* autonomy—in order to secure their stature in the abandoned primary world.

Perhaps I am getting ahead of myself. Critics agree that the second world functions for Hal in relation to his position in the primary world, but not that the second world as a whole functions in relation to the primary world, that the second world develops from the initial contents of the drama. Many see the second world as a separate, autonomous world of holiday retreat, which the

Prince enters and uses, in contradiction with the ethos of timelessness and charity that predominates in the tavern. This view, in effect, identifies the tavern as "Falstaff's world", and postulates an absolute opposition between Falstaff and the Prince. Falstaff, some argue, represents the spirit of good-fellowship or, at worst, anarchy and irresponsibility, qualities that the Prince, representative of hierarchy, authority, and responsibility, associates with but learns to dominate and (in *2 Henry IV*) to control. This argument puts forward two major misalignments: (1) it identifies Falstaff's character with his environment and (2) it creates a false antithesis between Hal's and Falstaff's motives within the tavern environment. To take and dispose of the first fallacy first: the charity and anarchy that Falstaff so heartily espouses characterize Falstaff but not the tavern itself, in that his charity comes out of others' pockets. In Falstaff's pockets we find only bills for his unpaid debts—and he tries to win compensation when even his bills are stolen (III. iii. 52ff.). In fact the tavern, as we see again and again from the point of view of the ostlers, carriers, vintner, drawers, and hostess, very much exists within an everyday world of time, work, and responsibility. By living there, Falstaff creates a continuous tension between the needs of his own ego, which he projects outward onto his environment, and the needs of the environment, which inevitably requires payment for services rendered.

I might add that the Prince, in so far as he "hast paid all" Falstaff's "part" (I. ii. 51–2), keeps this tension in solution: he allows Falstaff to continue to use and to impose himself on the everyday world of the tavern. By allowing this, by clearing the way for Falstaff's ego, Hal maintains a continuity between his behaviour and Falstaff's. Both Falstaff and Hal "use" rather than inhabit the tavern: the sentimental interpretation of *1 Henry IV*, according to which the tavern represents the ways of merry olde England, now threatened by the Lancastrian (or Tudor?) modern political state, although discredited, exists vestigially in the interpretations that oppose Falstaff's carefree "life" in the tavern to Hal's calculated "use" of the tavern. Falstaff, too, retreats to the tavern and uses it; Falstaff, unlike a Francis, goes to and dwells in the tavern by conscious choice, and, as with the Prince, in contradistinction to the privileges and responsibilities implicit in his rank or title.

Falstaff seems to use the tavern as a vantage from which to oppose the images and institutions of authority: he argues that he is governed by the moon, rather than by the standard image of royal authority, the sun (I. ii. 23 – 5); he identifies the sun not with a stable image of central authority, but with instability, immaturity, and popular romance, with "Phoebus, he, 'that wand'ring knight so fair'" (15 – 16); and, ultimately, he robs not pilgrims or traders, as he had originally planned to do, but men carrying "money of the King's . . . 'tis going to the King's exchequer" (II. ii. 54 – 5). But Falstaff's position in relation to authority shifts as the play develops; he later is incorporated into the highest ranks of the King's army, and he joins with the central monarchy to combat the threat to the government raised by the rebel forces. The contours of Falstaff's shift in attitude—from rebel against to associate of the King—follow the superficial outline of the Prince's movement and development, at least as discerned by those not in the know (or, not in the audience). But we know that the Prince's "reformation", in fact, unfolds a deeper consistency in his behaviour; can the same thing be true of Falstaff? does his final association with the state actually express the deeper contents of his initial opposition and of his supposed decadence?

Evidently, *I* think so; and I think we can get to this consistency of Falstaff's if, while keeping in mind the fundamental similarity between Falstaff and the Prince, we also keep in mind a distinction: opposing authority and opposing the state are not identical oppositions. The rebel forces, for example, oppose the state (not just as represented by King Henry; they want to divide the kingdom itself among themselves) without opposing the principles of authority. Falstaff, it seems, opposes authority, and he uses his initial opposition to the state, as he uses his later opposition to the rebels, in order to do so. But Falstaff's opposition to authority needs qualification, for it is based neither on principle nor on temperament, but on predicament. Falstaff opposes only the forces of authority that place limits on his own autonomy, whereas he works to maintain and uphold *his* authority—the autonomy of the ego—within the delimited environment of the tavern. Falstaff, like the Prince, uses the tavern as a form of or a place for work.

As Falstaff rebels against the institutions of authority he also rebels against his own decadence; we see this most clearly during the robbery at Gadshill. That episode begins with a series of jokes—some Hal's, some Falstaff's own—that associate Falstaff's hugeness with his death, or with images of death:

> If I travel but four foot by the squier further afoot, I shall break my wind. Well, I doubt not but to die a fair death for all this . . . ; (II. ii. 12—14)
>
> I'll starve ere I'll rob a foot further; (21—2)
>
> Eight yards of uneven ground is threescore and ten miles afoot with me, and the stony-hearted villains know it well enough; (24—7)
>
> Prince: Peace ye fat-guts, lie down. Lay thine ear close to the ground, and list if thou canst hear the tread of travellers.
> Falstaff: Have you any levers to lift me up again, being down? (31—5)

But Falstaff uses the occasion of the robbery, in effect, to turn these jokes around, to free himself from his own deathly vices by projecting them out into the world, onto others. Shakespeare subtly establishes the victims of the robbery as Falstaff's precise opposites: whereas Falstaff complains about walking and yearns for his horse, the first traveller enters saying:

> Come, neighbor, the boy shall lead our horses down the hill. We'll walk afoot a while, and ease our legs. (II. ii. 78—80)

The reverent, almost petit-bourgeois concerns for their posterity that the travellers express in their cries of anguish—"Jesu bless us!", "O, we are undone, both we and ours forever!" (82, 86—7)—directly oppose the blasphemous and violent exclamations with which Falstaff had anticipated the robbery: "Poins! Poins, and be hang'd!", " 'Zounds, will they not rob us?", "Now cannot I strike him, if I should be hang'd" (4, 65, 73). Falstaff, however, does not exactly respond to the travellers as moral opposites; he associates them with authority, the state, and the law—"You are grand-jurors, are ye? We'll jure ye, faith", (91—2)—but in the balance of his reaction to or attack on them he projects onto his victims his own agedness and his gluttonous appetite:

Ah, whoreson caterpillars! bacon-fed knaves! they hate us youth! (II. ii. 84—5)

Hang ye, gorbellied knaves, are ye undone? No, ye fat chuffs, I would your store were here! On, bacons, on! What, ye knaves, young men must live! (88—91)

The projection, of course, also creates a reversal: as the travellers become old and fat, Falstaff identifies himself with "us youth", and he becomes, it seems, suddenly quite mobile and agile. By projecting his vices, he also purges himself; when he binds the travellers (s. d. 92), he frees himself—from those aspects of his decadence that threaten his life.

Although the battle at Shrewsbury reverses Falstaff's initial opposition to the official representatives of authority, the battle also recapitulates some elements of the Gadshill robbery: Hal will rob Percy of his youth, instead of Falstaff of his purse; Falstaff will once again be on foot instead of on horseback, a position that he receives almost in response to his expressed wish that Hal rob the King:

Falstaff: Rob me the exchequer the first thing thou doest, and
           do it with unwash'd hands too.
Bardolph: Do, my lord.
Prince: I have procur'd thee, Jack, a charge of foot.
                              (III. iii. 183—6)

Note, however, that the Gadshill robbery ended when Falstaff bound the fat grandjurors, whereas Falstaff approaches the battle at Shrewsbury with emaciated recruits—"such scarecrows"—whom he has freed from the bondage of prison (IV. ii. 38—42). Having joined forces with the state, Falstaff no longer need bind his vices; in fact, he uses the battle, as he had earlier used the tavern, as an opportunity to extend and expand his gluttony. Falstaff speaks of the battlefield in terms of a tavern ("I fear the shot here, here's no scoring but upon the pate" V. iii. 30—1), leads his soldiers to where they are "pepper'd" (36), carries a bottle of sack in his pistol case (53—4), and imagines the dead and wounded bodies, even his own, as meat for grilling, as "carbonado[es]" (58). Falstaff can release his vices, his appetite, during the battle not because he has changed but because, during war, the state itself changes its attitude toward its subjects. Throughout the play Falstaff's gluttony remains a constant, but, by the time of the battle, it no longer acts as a liability; rather, gluttony aligns Falstaff with the official policies of the state. During the battle, soldiers become, in Falstaff's apt phrasing, "food for powder" (IV. ii. 65–6); when Hal tries to make Falstaff's recruits into objects of pity, "such pitiful rascals", Falstaff corrects Hal's attitude with his ghastly pun: his recruits are things, without stature or quality, things that will "fill a pit as well as better" (66–7).

The state itself becomes gluttonous, however, as a phase within its process of reorganization or, to apply Henry's identification of the state with the sick body of the King, rehabilitation. By reducing people into objects, the state temporarily abandons its social stratifications in order to make the social hierarchy, when re-established, more stable and secure. Similarly, during battle, the rigors of physical combat supercede such "everyday" ethical and civil abstractions as courtesy only so that, after the battle, other abstractions, such as honour, become the measure of stature. Consequently, the King and Prince, triumphant in the battle, do not emerge as identical with the forces of gluttony that the battle released; on the contrary: after the battle the royal family behaves with greater courtesy, control, and sanctimonious piety than ever before:

> Ill-spirited Worcester, did not we send grace,
> Pardon, and terms of love to all of you?
> And wouldst thou turn our offers contrary?
> Misuse the tenor of thy kinsman's trust? (V. v. 2–5)

By using gluttony during crisis the monarchy can, the crisis having passed, identify itself as the antithesis of gluttony, as the representatives of patience, fair adjudication, and virtue rewarded.

Just as the state adopts the gluttonous policies of war during a period of crisis, of external threat to its political institutions and conditions, only the individual without a stable and secure position of authority tries to increase his stature through gluttony, the immediate consumption of and the treatment of abstract qualities as material objects. The physical appearances of the characters emblematically represent this opposition between those with and without authority: whereas Falstaff the glutton is swollen, blown out, gross, both Hal and Henry, the figures of authority, are, according to both themselves and others, shaken, pale, and drawn. Falstaff's ravenous consumption of food and drink matches Hotspur's aggressive consumption of honourable deeds (which Hal's imagination associates with eating a hearty breakfast, II. iv. 101–5). Those without authority devour whatever is set before them. Those with authority, however, can plan things out and look ahead, and consequently they need not be the slaves to appetite; they can store away food for later use, just as they can, by objectifying themselves, hoard up parts of their own personalities and, by objectifying others, accumulate the good deeds or misdeeds of their companions and their opponents. To the extent that Falstaff anticipates social elevation after his "success" in battle, he prepares to relinquish his need for immediate consumption and, consequently, to give up his body along with his gluttony: "If I do grow great, I'll grow less, for I'll purge and leave sack, and live cleanly as a nobleman should do" (V. iv. 163–5). (Slenderness, for Falstaff, involves a fantasy of being completely embraced by a symbol of wealth and authority. He reminisces: "I was not an eagle's talent in the waist, I could have crept into any alderman's thumb-ring", II. iv. 30–1) Falstaff's last words in the play, his fantasy of a simultaneous loss of weight and gain in stature, recall the familiar pastoral paradox—take less, have more—but they also place the pastoral attitude in the correct causal sequence: the pastoral protagonist does not take less and thereby have more, but, having more, he or she can afford, at any given moment, to take less.

Both Hal and Falstaff make use of their environments, but in different ways and with differing implications. The distinction between Falstaff's immediate consumption and Hal's accumulation marks an opposition between two attitudes toward the self as a participant in history. Falstaffian immediate consumption obliterates all time into a continuous present and thereby denies the self access to historical process. The non-historicity of appetite, of immediate consumption, if allowed to become a permanent or dominant condition, actually threatens the existence of established authority, in that the legitimacy, hence the power, of the institutions of the state depend on historicity, on the established and felt legal or traditional connections between current and past institutions and on the implied continuity from current to future institutions and figures. The continuous present of appetite can align itself with the ideals of the state during battle, but afterwards, once the state itself ceases to *use* gluttony, the principles of appetite directly contradict the principles of tradition, inheritance, and legacy on which the state depends. Although Falstaff himself does not become antagonistic to the state itself in this play, both Prince and King use such accumulative strategies as delay and calculation to obliterate the continuous present of appetite, of Falstaffian gluttony, to demonstrate that actions taken in the present have implications for actions in the past and of the future. The Lancastrian strategy of accumulation requires heightened consciousness of history, in that setting something aside implies a faith in the future, just as redeeming implies a knowledge of the past. The King and Prince show that people can participate in and, through effort, can control historical processes. To exert this control over history, people need a way of quantifying the abstract relations they as participants hold to past and future. *Henry IV, Part One*, expresses this quantified relationship as the consciousness of time.

"TO DEMAND THE TIME OF DAY" *Prince Hal*

From his first moment on stage Hal disputes Falstaff's need, even his right, to know the time:

> Falstaff: Now, Hal, what time of day is it, lad?
> Hal: . . . What a devil hast thou to do with the time of day? unless hours were cups of sack, and minutes capons, and clocks the tongues of bawds, and dials the signs of leaping-houses, and the blessed sun himself a fair hot wench in flame-color'd taffata; I see no reason why thou shouldst be so superfluous to demand the time of day. (I. ii. 1–12)

Hal responds more vehemently than the contents of Falstaff's request demand, indicating, as Roy Battenhouse has pointed out, that Falstaff has raised both a question and an issue.[1] Falstaff's question about the time of day seems to encroach upon Hal's territory; Hal frightens Falstaff off as he might a poacher or a trespasser—the Prince needs to maintain a boundary and a difference between himself and Falstaff. Hal here asserts and imposes the boundary between knowing and not knowing (perhaps between caring and not caring about) the time of day, but the terms through which Hal suggests Falstaff's indifference to time give the boundary between Hal and Falstaff a set of secondary meanings. By suggesting that Falstaff's interest in time—in anything—must be material, Hal accuses Falstaff of an inability to think in abstractions. He creates an image of a Falstaff obsessed with lust, gluttony, and debauchery, and, in doing so, Hal defends himself. Hal protects himself by proposing that, for Falstaff, concern with the time of day becomes obliterated in the continuous present of gluttonous satisfaction; Hal's own historical identity as part of a family of Machiavells, without legitimate title to the crown, is projected onto another's identity, is transformed from political into corporeal gluttony. By creating and then projecting the association of not knowing the time with debauchery and immediate consumption, Hal can maintain for himself the assurance that so long as he does know the time he will be free from Falstaffian contagion, he will be able to delay gratification and thereby control his environment and his destiny, his place in history. Hal never answers Falstaff's question.

Nor does Falstaff demand an answer. Instead of pursuing his initial question, Falstaff adopts the Prince's verbal strategy of self-defense through polar opposition. He accepts indifference to the time of day and asserts dedication to the night, calling himself a man "of good government, being govern'd, as the sea is, by our noble and chaste mistress the moon" (27–9). This retort has left Hal vulnerable; should the Prince still wish to maintain his opposition to Falstaff, he would have to develop a defense of the day's beauty, which for some reason he does not do—perhaps because defending the beauty of the sun would come too close, metaphorically, to a defense of the King's government, an argument he will not risk losing. Instead, Hal shifts ground and pronouns entirely, as he includes himself in Falstaff's image cluster of thievery, government, sun, and moon:

Thou sayest well, and it holds well too, for the fortune of *us* that are the moon's men doth ebb and flow like the sea, being govern'd, as the sea is, by the moon. (I. ii. 30–3)

With this shift from Falstaffian opponent to Falstaffian associate the Prince shows us for the first time in the play his much-noted ambiguity, or, in the perhaps more appropriate term, ambivalence (the one term describes Shakespeare's motivation; the other, Hal's). Hal dissociates himself from, because he feels repulsed by, the materiality and sensuality of Falstaff's sense of time, which measures by appetite and desire, but Hal does not carry this attitude to its logical conclusion, he does not claim to represent and uphold the abstract time of history. Hal's ambivalence allows him to join with Falstaff in attacking authority—"the day's beauty"—while never binding himself to appetite, "the night's body".

Through the two sides of his attitude toward indulgence, Hal enacts within the tavern his ambivalent relation to authority. Hal uses the tavern so as to indulge his carnal and corporeal appetites—for food, drink, and perhaps sex, depending on what one means by calling the hostess of the tavern "to a reckoning many a time and oft" (49–50)—while he describes his life at the tavern as not a holiday interlude but a period of work and austerity reluctantly undertaken so as to consolidate and fortify his social stature within the primary world of history. Prince Hal, like other aristocratic protagonists, uses the second world as part of his strategy for maintaining authority in the primary world, but he does not accept the tavern as a retreat, a holiday interlude. He consciously opposes the intimations of timelessness and of charity with his own sense of hierarchy and propriety and with his cognizance of time. Hal, more conscious of the political function of retreat than the aristocratic protagonists in the double-world comedies, uses the tavern as a functioning term within the world of history. Hal maintains his own authority in the midst of indulgence rather than perpetrate the fiction that indulgence temporarily releases a whole society from the need for authority.

But the aristocratic authority that Hal maintains in the tavern does not entirely oppose him to all those without aristocratic stature. Hal's maintained authority does have *some* advantages for Falstaff, at least in so far as Hal has "credit" enough to have "paid all" Falstaff's "part" (51–8). The aristocratic credit Hal gains through his authority relieves him of obligation to Falstaff and obliges him to acknowledge implicitly his historical, his future, responsibilities as the Prince. Hal can both answer and not answer Falstaff's question about the time—he can reproach Falstaff for not needing to know without suggesting that he himself knows the time—but, because Falstaff knows the difference in stature between himself and the Prince, as well as the advantages and dangers which that difference contains for him, he can both ask and not ask his question. Falstaff's question, therefore, contains an element of reproach, as if he means to taunt Hal for not knowing the time, to remind Hal that he has become dangerously close to an existence within the continuous present of appetite: "Indeed you come near me now, Hal" (13).

Falstaff repeats this reproach, adopting Hal's turn of phrase, later in the play when the two meet near Coventry on their way to battle. "What a devil dost thou in Warwickshire?", Falstaff asks the Prince; then, turning to the Lord of Westmoreland, who accompanies the Prince to the battlefield, Falstaff adds: "I thought your honor had already been at Shrewsbury" (IV. ii. 50−3). Here, of course, Falstaff subtly but significantly reverses the terms and positions employed in his initial exchange with Hal. Falstaff now directly suggests that Hal has no concern with the time; he intimates that Hal has again "come near" him by delaying his approach to the battle, by lagging behind in the safety of Coventry while Percy "is already in the field" (75). Although Falstaff's intimations about Hal's sense of historical responsibility have become quite direct—they approach accusation—Hal, in contrast with his vehement response during their first discussion about the time, responds to Falstaff with measured restraint and good-natured wit. In fact, Westmoreland parries Falstaff's thrust:

Faith, Sir John, 'tis more than time that I were there [i.e. at Shrewsbury], and you too, but my powers are there already.

(IV. ii. 54−6)

Although the Prince, too, encourages Falstaff to "make haste" (74), I think that Hal's consciousness has been divided. He has, by this point in the play, overcome his *dramatic* ambivalence toward the world of appetite, the tavern, but he cannot yet declare his resolution, perhaps because of the *moral* ambivalence, his combined sense of compassion and contempt for Falstaff's soldiers, that he maintains. Consequently, the official and historical side of Hal's consciousness, that part of Hal that uses the tavern for work rather than for indulgence, gets, in this scene, displaced onto the otherwise entirely superfluous Lord of Westmoreland. This displacement prevents Falstaff from knowing how conscious Hal has become of historical time and of his place in history; Falstaff, and to some extent the audience, therefore perceives the two sides of Hal's attitude toward history, toward the battle, as the attitudes of two different people. Both Shakespeare and Hal use the Lord of Westmoreland: Shakespeare uses him to prevent Falstaff from too early experiencing his separation from the Prince; Hal uses him as an official spokesman, one who will enunciate the official and public policies that Hal has agreed to support but behind whom Hal can continue, when appropriate or advantageous, to jest and dally.

Hal's delegation to the Lord of Westmoreland of a portion of his public voice signifies both the authority that Hal maintains regarding other public figures in the drama (Hal and his father are the only characters who can successfully partition their own consciousnesses) and the bifold problem that confronts the Prince each time history, through the regulations of the court, intervenes in the tavern. I call Hal's problem bifold because it has two separate and separable aspects: Hal must both commit himself to eventual participation in the world of historical time and he must determine when and how others, in court and tavern, will become aware that he understands his own responsibilities and that he has the capacity for action.

These two issues converge immediately after Hal's play-acting scene with Falstaff, as the sheriff, representing the authority inherent in the kingdom, enters the tavern. Hal has just, in his famous response to Falstaff's impassioned self-defense, declared both his present and eventual separation from Falstaff's sensual indulgences; I believe, however, that Hal says "I do, I will" (II. iv. 481) as a burst of dramatic bravura: I doubt the Prince should really consciously control his destiny here, for he continues in the high spirits of good fellowship until the entry of the law. (Perhaps Falstaff somehow realizes the implications of Hal's outburst, and thus takes refuge from destiny in the primal narcissism of drunken sleep.) But Hal changes when the sheriff and the carrier come on stage; quite literally, Hal's words become good. He stops the sheriff, who is pursuing a "well known" man whom he "hath followed . . . unto this house" (II. iv. 506–10), by giving assurance, by giving his word:

The man I do assure you is not here,
For I myself at this time have employ'd him.
And, sheriff, I will engage my word to thee
That I will by to-morrow dinner-time
Send him to answer thee, . . . (II. iv. 512–16)

Here we see one instance of the credit through which Hal has paid
Falstaff's part; Hal earns the credit by his aristocratic mastery of
language. Hal's word is good because his speech is good.
Shakespeare very deftly allows Hal's cadences to control the
actions of others. Hal's gradual shift into blank verse seems to bring
the sheriff up short, to catch him by surprise and to force him to
measure out the contents of his inquiry. Hal greets the sheriff in
slightly irregular pentametre:

Now, Master Sheriff, what is your will with me? (506)

to which the sheriff responds in more regulated verse:

First, pardon me, my lord. A hue and cry
Hath followed certain men unto this house. (507–8)

Here Hal breaks the measure, interjecting his question—"What
men?" (509)—which may mistakenly lead the sheriff and carrier
to feel that, their inquiry having approached Hal's guilt, he has
begun to let the measure of his language slip from his control. The
sheriff, however, answers Hal in formal metre:

One of them is well known, my gracious lord,
A gross fat man. (II. iv. 510–11)

(He has avoided saying that another one of them also is well
known—the Prince himself.) The formality of his description of
Falstaff gets debased by the carrier's irregular prose interjection:
"As fat as butter" (511).

Ordinarily Hal would take the carrier's opening and respond in
kind, with another metaphor about Falstaff's grossness. (At
Coventry he, too, calls Falstaff "butter".) Instead, he responds in
seven lines of formal, almost perfectly regular, pentameter, from
which I have quoted above ("The man I do assure you . . ."). Hal

completes his elegant passage by asking the sheriff to "Leave the house," (518) to which the sheriff humbly replies:

> I will, my lord. There are two gentlemen
> Have in this robbery lost three hundred marks.
> (II. iv. 519—20)

Hal of course must be informed of every point of the charge against the men the sheriff is seeking, but notice how the sheriff makes the active element of the charge the gentlemen who have "lost" the marks "in this robbery" and not the men who might have been said to have robbed the gentlemen. Hal's reply, however, takes on (or at least delegates to Falstaff) full active responsibility for robbing the men. In doing so, Hal, metrically, almost duplicates the sheriff's couplet, with the full stop occurring exactly at the same point:

> It may be so. If he have robb'd these men,
> He shall be answerable, and so farewell. (II. iv. 521—2)

The sheriff bids farewell to Hal with three iambs—"Good night, my noble lord", (523). This line of verse seems to ask to be completed by Hal with two more iambs or even dactyls, such as "Good night, sheriff". Instead, Hal responds with an independent line of pentameter:

> I think it is good morrow, is it not? (524)

Hal's response thoroughly surprises everyone, both because of its metrical independence from the context and because of the direct message it contains. By this one rather gracious line the Prince suggests that he can step away from his environment—metrical, dramatic, and social—and initiate new patterns of control. Further, and more important, the Prince has declared aloud—to the sheriff, to the audience, and to anyone lurking in the wings or backstage—that he can separate himself from the world of continuous revelry, the constant present of appetite, that he can discriminate among different times, and that he can use and discuss time as a process and, perhaps, as a force connected with history and responsibility. In short, Hal, at this crux in the drama, responds to Falstaff's question; he informs Falstaff and the sheriff that he knows the time of day.

We may assume that Hal's resolute control and his prescience take the sheriff aback ("Indeed, my lord, I think it be two a'clock", 525); Falstaff, however, "fast asleep behind the arras" (528), has missed Hal's performance, which may in part account for the rage, the overt death-wish, that, as M. D. Faber has noted, Hal expresses toward Falstaff when his sleeping and snorting body is revealed.[2] The Prince contrasts Falstaff's gluttony and indebtedness with his own implicit accumulation and, in keeping with the metaphor he had privately established earlier, in his soliloquy, with repayment of "the debt [he] never promised", (I. ii. 209). The debt, of course, works on two levels: "the money shall be paid back again with advantage" (II. iv. 547–8), but also the Prince will go "to the court in the morning" (543–4), and they "must all to the wars" (544). He (they all?) will redeem Hal's dissolute life in the tavern by serving the King in battle. Hal employs the debt metaphor again during his greatest trial in battle; as he saves his father's life, he claims that he, as Prince of Wales, if perhaps not as Hal of Eastcheap, "never promiseth but he means to pay". After Hal has made good his promise, the King commends him: "Thou has *redeem'd* thy lost opinion, /And show'd thou mak'st *some tender* of my life", (V. iv. 43, 48–9). Hal prepares himself to pay back with his body his indebtedness to a force outside of his body, a force that, during the battle at Shrewsbury, comes to be represented by the body, or the life within the body, of his father, the King. This kind of indebtedness and compensation separates the Prince from Falstaff, who, as his "papers" show, remains indebted to the force of appetite, which of course has come to be represented by his own body. The differentiation between Hal and Falstaff degenerates into animosity, and further accounts for Hal's barely disguised aggression toward Falstaff ("I know his death will be a march of twelve score" II. iv. 546–7).

Differentiation becomes animosity because Falstaff functions as Hal's antagonist as well as as his "foil", although Hal does not make that discovery until the particular convergence of events that the sheriff's arrival precipitated. Hal's conscious control of the present through his metrical dominance of the dialogue, his forthright public declaration that he knows the time, followed by his exposé of Falstaff's complete indifference to debts, time, and the state, dramatize, in a way that the rhetoric of Hal's initial soliloquy cannot, the separation between Hal's consciousness of his environment and Falstaff's enclosure within the needs and boundaries of his ego. But Hal does not experience this separation as an absolute opposition. The Prince associates himself with Falstaffian egoism as part of what he considers a temporary denial and a period of austerity, but Hal uses this association with another's indulgences in order eventually to extend greatly his capacity for action within history, for satisfaction of his greater Machiavellian appetite for political power within the realm.

"REVOLTED TAPSTERS, AND OSTLERS TRADE-FALL'N"

In his soliloquy (I. ii. 195–217) Hal introduces the two themes or goals—being himself and redeeming the time—that will dominate both his own consciousness and the dramatic action for the rest of the play. Hal plans to achieve these goals (he has no doubt, by the way, that his true "self" is the Prince of Wales) by a strategy that will "falsify men's hopes"; he will make the public think of and expect so little from him that when he eventually makes known his true if unexceptional royal qualities his "reformation" will make what would have been merely the expected or normative behaviour appear heroic. This has always seemed to me pretty bad reasoning; in our own time the public has never forgiven those political figures with dissolute or dishonourable pasts—we tend to look to the past for evidence not of reformation but of tainted character—and I doubt that this phenomenon developed only recently. Still, I do not think we can simply say that Hal's belief that dissoluteness will offer him political advantages merely serves as a rationale, a way of permitting himself simultaneously the indulgence of appetite and the restraint of historical responsibility. His ambivalence develops not just because he wants it both ways, but because he feels both ways about the tavern itself. The descriptive images he selects—the "base contagious clouds", the foul and ugly mists" that "smother up his beauty", that "seem to strangle him" (I. ii. 198, 202, 199, 203)—reveal his contempt of and disdain for his associates within the tavern.

Much of the confusion about Hal's attitude toward the tavern has developed because of the particular metaphor he chooses to explain or illustrate the political advantages he will gain by his dissolute retreat:

> If all the year were playing holidays,
> To sport would be as tedious as to work;
> But when they seldom come, they wish'd for come,
> And nothing pleaseth but rare accidents. (I. ii. 204—7)

Because so many, for reasons sentimental or critical, would like to see Hal's sojourn at Eastcheap either as a period of comic or holiday regeneration[3] or else as a period of misrule during which the Prince learns to communicate with all social classes in the realm,[4] Hal's soliloquy has been cited as evidence that he sees the world of Eastcheap as a "playing" holiday but that he, maturely, realizes that continuous holiday would become boring, from which we can infer that Hal intends to return "to work", to his princely responsibilities. He may intend to do so, but in analyzing the holiday/everyday antithesis we must not let the ramifications of Hal's holiday metaphor, so important in Shakespeare's comedies, as C. L. Barber has shown, distract us from what Hal actually says. Hal actually uses the holiday/everyday antithesis as further development of the "being wanted, he may be more wond'red at" (201) theme, of which the sun emerging from the clouds constitutes the first instance. Hal's metaphor actually declares that his life in the tavern correlates to or represents the "tedious" world of everyday, of work, but that when he emerges and assumes responsibility, pays his "debt", the feeling of relief, presumably among the English people, will feel like the relief from the tedium of work created by a holiday, especially an unexpected one. Others will wish for Hal's return to authority, to *his* everyday of work, as they would wish for their own seldom-coming holidays, their own *release* from work. In short, Hal invokes the holiday/everyday antithesis to associate his indulgences in the tavern with the feeling, among others, of everyday work, and thereby to transform his own supposed holiday at Eastcheap into an occupation.

It is convenient for the Prince, and characteristic of him, to invert the poles of holiday and everyday, to suggest, even though only metaphorically, that what might seem pure indulgence actually, when seen from another perspective, constitutes a princely form of tedious work. By creating for us this double vision of the world of the tavern, forcing the audience to see the tavern as retreat from time and responsibility but also as the Prince's work, Hal formulates an ambiguous and privileged attitude toward holiday. Because Hal has redefined his "idleness" as a form of work, the tavern inactivity cannot be completely associated with charity and appetite nor can it be dissociated from hierarchy and history. Hal's indulgence in the tavern idleness, a period during which the Prince unyokes his humour to join with Falstaff in the abolition of the sense of time and in the pursuit of gratification of the appetites, cannot go so far as to establish a period of misrule, of abolition or inversion of social degree. Prince Hal's idleness establishes in the tavern only the temporary predominance of appetite; since he uses appetite to secure eventually his own aristocratic position, he cannot include along with his version of holiday the traditional charity, equality, and inversion of social hierarchy.

In fact, the Prince's relationship to the tavern, by enacting only one aspect of holiday, inverts the traditional attitude holiday creates toward social degree and hierarchy. Instead of dissolving his set of personal and professional associations into a brotherhood of good men's feasts, Hal exaggerates the difference in stature between himself and the others in his environment. Because Prince Hal uses indulgence as a political strategy and gratification of the appetites as a form of his work, his particular use of the tavern environment exaggerates the social difference between the Prince and those who work to satisfy the appetites of others. The tavern setting perfectly dramatizes this differentiation, for the tavern employees work by serving their patrons' appetites; Hal's soliloquy, in effect, claims that they also serve who only stand and wait. Perhaps—if we limit our interpretation of *1 Henry IV* to Hal's aristocratic point of view; but the play forces us to interpret Hal's attempt to be himself and to redeem the time within a complex of everyday activities undertaken by members of different social classes with different and sometimes antagonistic functions and attitudes.

The somewhat puzzling scene (II. iv. 1—112) with Francis the drawer functions primarily, I think, to document for us the effect Hal's holiday retreat has on the life of the tavern and to show the attitude toward servants Hal must adopt and maintain so as to secure his status as a member of the ruling class. I disagree with those readers who have taken Hal at his word ("I am sworn brother to leash of drawers . . . I am so good a proficient in one quarter of an hour, that I can drink with any tinker in his own language during my life", 6– 20) and argued that in the tavern Hal learns to communicate with people of all degrees, and thereby improves his ability eventually to rule with fairness and compassion. E. M. W. Tillyard, for example, defends Hal's cruelty and condescension toward the drawers by arguing that it must be "taken for granted" that in Shakespeare's time "the subhuman element [i.e. Francis and the other drawers!] in the population . . . should be treated almost like beasts". [5] I consider that Hal's condescension ("I have sounded the very base-string of humility", 5– 6) if not his contempt, as he associates the drawers with beasts (a "leash") and with inanimate objects ("three or four loggerheads amongst three or four hogsheads", 4– 5) become quite obvious during this scene. Perhaps less apparent than his condescension, Hal's actual ignorance and limitation develop not because of any deficiency in his character but because of the stratification in the tavern society. Hal claims sworn brotherhood with the drawers, and he bases his claim partially on his knowledge of their language. Hal's security in claiming to be able to "drink with any tinker in his own language" derives from his mistaken belief in the drawers' linguistic deficiency; he believes that at least one of them:

> never spake other English in his life than "Eight shillings and sixpence", and "You are welcome", with this shrill addition, "Anon, anon, sir! Score a pint of bastard in the Halfmoon", or so. (II. iv. 24– 8)

Hal, though, reports subjectively on the drawers' language; his own aristocratic limitations of vision distort his observations. Hal's preposterous claim to have become a linguistic expert or a cultural anthropologist in fifteen minutes fails to account for what might be called the cultural application of the uncertainty principle: the limitations in the language of the drawers occur only when they speak in the presence of an outside observer, especially an observer of superior social rank. Hal cannot observe the drawers in isolation, so his presence must dynamically affect the nature of the language that he learns.

Although Hal remains unaware that environment influences language, while he questions Francis "to drive away the time" (28) we become quite conscious of the interdependence of language and social status. S. P. Zitner, who sees the jest as Hal's "imaginative projection of his own fate into the fate of Francis" (69) has compared Francis's dilemma, whether to speak with the Prince or to "look to the guests within", (81) with Hal's, whether to confront Percy or to bide his time;[6] although the two dilemmas do have similar structures, they have vastly different contents. Once we look past the structure and see the class contents that inform both Hal's and Francis's relations to their environments, we see that the difference between these two figures *"not knowing which way to go"* (s.d. 79) far outweighs their similarities. Hal has voluntarily adopted a temporary position of stasis between alternatives; Hal's stasis within the tavern derives from the authority he brings to the tavern. Through the jest against Francis, Hal manifests this authority: the jest demonstrates Hal's ability to set up a scene or, in a wider, sense, to make a world. Francis constitutes a part of the world that Hal creates to drive away the time till Falstaff comes, but Francis does not know exactly what kind of a world Hal is creating out of him; he does not know the boundaries of the world. Because of this, Francis creates the dilemma for himself: he believes that he must choose between eventual service to the Prince and immediate service to the patron (Poins) calling offstage.

Had Francis realized that the Prince's world extends offstage to include Poins's calling, he would have known that there was no choice to be made at all. From a dramatic standpoint, Francis's limited perspective makes it impossible for him to realize that the bellowing Poins and the beguiling Prince are both participating in the same "action". From a social standpoint, however, the scene demonstrates to the audience that service to a better master can never equal freedom, a lesson that Caliban learns in a different context. Francis's tentative efforts at social elevation actually intensify his humiliation and his subjection; Francis's partial acquiescence to Hal's offer of freedom accentuates his indentured service, which Francis performs by catering to the appetites of the "guests within". Francis mistakenly believes that Hal could possibly perceive him as something other than pure object.

As in the comic second worlds, the aristocratic protagonist in Eastcheap transforms people into objects within the landscape, things present to serve his own subjective needs. In Shakespeare's comedies, this objectification takes many different forms: Duke Senior gets pleasure seeing Jaques's melancholy, Orsino uses Viola's love for him to get her to woo (and win) Olivia's love. In 1 *Henry IV*, in the context of the entire play, the Prince's use of Francis, although incidental, focuses our attention on Hal's ambivalence toward the tavern. By pretending to know Francis's language while doing everything he can to retain, if not intensify, his aristocratic view of Francis the servant as pure object, Hal incorporates into the tavern holiday without charity, an indulgence dependent on stature.

The Prince does not realize that the apparently comic limitations of Francis's vocabulary—"That ever this fellow should have fewer words than a parrot, and yet be the son of a woman!" (98–9)—result entirely from the service Francis is called upon to perform. His labour in the tavern requires his conscious limitation of his language, as the Prince's jest amply demonstrates. For Francis to try to engage in conversation, he must ignore his occupation, his "calling", and in doing so run an evident risk, as the entry of the vintner demonstrates. This tableau, in which the Prince mocks Francis's linguistic limitation—the precise limitation that the imposed servitude of the Prince's jest ensures—while Francis struggles to show the Prince, perhaps for the first time, that he can speak, creates as clear a picture as any of Shakespeare's understanding of class relationships in the tavern and elsewhere. For completion, this picture needs some final touches in its dramatic and linguistic background, which Shakespeare provides in the mysterious opening of Act II, the scene with the two carriers. By opening the robbery episode with the conversation, rich with slang and jargon, between the two carriers, Shakespeare has extended the linguistic range of the play. We hear servingmen talking to each other, without the modulating presence of an aristocratic observer, without, at first, the conscious limitation imposed by explicit demands for service. In contrast to Hal's report on the language of the drawers, the carriers' language, although not eloquent, contains much verbal resource. The carriers have a rich, precise vocabulary, requiring numerous explicatory footnotes in any modern edition of the text; they speak with rough wit, imagery, examples, appropriate diction, and, I think, an amusingly flexible use of personal pronouns:

> They will allow us ne'er a jordan, and then we leak in your chimney, and your chamber-lye breeds fleas like a loach.
>
> (II. i. 19–21)

Although he might have had the carriers speak after the Prince ridicules Francis's linguistic deficiency, by introducing the carriers without apparent motive Shakespeare establishes the world of the tavern as one that encompasses all kinds of languages, thereby alerting us to the bias and improbability of the Prince's claims to have learned the language of the drawers, as well as to the extent that the Prince's social stature homogenizes, distorts, and censors the language and the dialect spoken in his presence.

Several devices stress the intentional if oblique connection between the carriers' and the Francis scenes. In the carriers' scene we hear the cry within of "Anon, anon" (4), which seems to punctuate the conversations at Eastcheap and which establishes an inverse continuity from the carriers to Francis. The first carrier precedes his conversation with the other carrier by asking Tom, a stableboy (without a speaking part), to "beat Cut's saddle, put a few flocks in the point" (5–6); similarly, Francis precedes his discussion with Hal by asking Ralph, presumably a young apprentice drawer (also without a speaking part—perhaps played by the same young apprentice actor?), to "look down into the Pomgarnet", (II. iv. 37–8). Both Francis and the carrier thus first appear while executing some authority within their limited spheres. Further, the conversations establish that Francis and the carrier perform, on different levels, the same function: each transports nourishment— "a gammon of bacon and two razes of ginger" (II. i. 24–5), turkeys, wine—while living themselves amid relative deprivation. Again, Shakespeare does not emphasize this, but in this play so concerned with appetite, he draws our attention to an association between those who carry the components of the feast from one place to another.

One additional line of continuity joins Francis and the carriers: each is asked "what's a' clock?" (II. i. 32; II. iv. 96). What enormous

significance that simple question acquires! The first carrier, unlike
Hal and Falstaff in their first appearance, when they argued about
the need to know—because neither of them knew—the time,
replies to Gadshill's question: "I think it be two o'clock". He uses
precisely the same words that, toward the end of the act and
presumably exactly twenty-four hours later, the sheriff speaks to
Hal, immediately before his "*Exit [with Carrier]*" (II. iv. s. d. 525).
The carrier's knowing the time recalls Hal's failure to answer
Falstaff's initial query about the time, which in itself is later
recalled when the Prince discusses the time of night, or morning,
with the placated sheriff.

It seems, then, that knowing and not knowing the time directly
correlates with responsibility and indulgence. But what about
Francis? We cannot say that he does not know the time; he ignores
Hal's question—"What's a' clock, Francis? Anon, anon, sir" (II. iv.
96−7)—because Hal catches him while totally involved in the
present: *anon*, of course, derives from "at once". But his involvement in the present differs from Falstaff's and Hal's indulgent
oblivion; Francis is consumed by present business, so that in a way
his not knowing the time also develops from his devotion to
responsibility. The tedium of Francis's responsibility forces his
oblivion of clock time (the carriers know clock time in part
because of this tedium, in that they work on a schedule and want
to reach London before daylight, II. i. 41−4) and ensures his
cognizance of calendar time. Had he been allowed to continue, he
could have told the Prince to the day how long he "hast . . . to
serve" (II. iv. 41−2). By not knowing the time of day, while
knowing, in a sense, the time of year, Francis adds a new term to
the opposition between indulgence and responsibility: Francis
cares about the time in so far as it can bring him freedom. To
achieve freedom he must either serve out his apprenticeship or get
a new master, bide his time or seize the time. Put another way,
Francis must choose whether to be a subject who acts or an object
acted upon.

This choice does not so much correlate with Prince Hal's as it
does with the choice already made by Henry IV. The first scene of
the play dramatizes the King's active, almost aggressive, attitude
toward time—"So shaken as we are, so wan with care, / Find we a
time for frighted peace to pant" (I. i. 1−2). As he makes clear
during his interview with the Prince, he has seized his place in

history; as his battle plans evince, he intends to retain his place in history by scrupulous attention to calendar time:

> The Earl of Westmerland set forth to-day
> With him my son, Lord John of Lancaster,
> For this advertisement is five days old.
> On Wednesday next, Harry, you shall set forward,
> On Thursday we ourselves will march. Our meeting
> Is Bridgenorth. And, Harry, you shall march
> Through Gloucestershire; by which account,
> Our business valued, some twelve days hence
> Our general forces at Bridgenorth shall meet.
> Our hands are full of business, let's away,
> Advantage feeds him fat while men delay. (III. ii. 170–80)

The King's closing image emphasizes the predominant oppositions in the play between the responsibility—the "business"—of history and the indulgence of appetite. (The next scene opens with Falstaff worried about having "wither'd" III. iii. 1–4, perhaps symbolically indicating that once the political forces of the kingdom unite in action, Falstaffian indulgence, the personal form of "advantage", can no longer "feed . . . him fat".) The King's actions, though, show us that responsibility, when exercised by the ruling classes, exactly opposes responsibility as exercised by the servants. The King's attention to time enables him to objectify the others—opponents, collaborators, family—in his environment. He has attained, and he maintains, his power by manipulating people and their opinions, by using people as props. This quality of mind ultimately gets dramatized on the battlefield, when "the King hath many marching in his coats" (V. iii. 25), when the King projects the objective symbols of his authority onto others in order to maintain for himself maximum freedom. The King fulfills historical responsibility by transforming his environment into a system of objects, which in turn leaves him the greatest possible freedom to act as a subject within history.

Francis, however, fulfills responsibility by being oblivious of time. He must serve the continuous present of appetite; to do so he must be willing to be perceived as much as possible as an object, devoid of subjectivity and consciousness. The Prince presents Francis with a dilemma by treating him simultaneously as both subject and object. Hal asks Francis to express his conscious feelings about freedom (and about time) in order to document the absolute limitation of Francis's language, of his consciousness. For Francis, the continual objecthood and limited consciousness through which he enacts his responsibility of service, whether to the vintner or, as he hopes, the Prince, fulfills his vision of freedom. This "interval" between Hal and Francis clarifies the crucial social opposition of 1 *Henry IV* by demonstrating that we cannot assert an absolute correspondence between historical responsibility and freedom; we cannot say that, because Hal releases himself from the false freedom of Falstaffian appetite into the true freedom of action that comes with accepting a role in history, the play documents a correspondence between freedom and responsibility. That correspondence exists only for those whose social stature enables them to place themselves as a subject within an environment and to see their environment as pure object, material for manipulation. The play shows that with increased social stature, accepting historical responsibility can become a more rarefied method of gratifying appetite.

Those without social stature accept history and responsibility by serving others' subjective needs, needs that in 1 *Henry IV* almost always are expressed through objects and metaphors of food and appetite. Those who serve can retain their own freedom and subjectivity only so long as they can maintain an awareness of the time. So long as the servant can be aware of a system of regulation, such as a wage structure, outside of or beyond the continuous present of an employer's appetite, he maintains an integrity and can be identified in part by his own need, not just by his service to the needs of another. In this sense, a wage labourer has relatively greater freedom than an indentured or a retained servant, which in part explains why members of the aristocracy, when forced into the role of servant (Orlando, Kent, Viola, e.g.) disdain those who work for wages. Francis, at least when in the presence of Hal, becomes mute, devoid of language and therefore of consciousness, because he hopes to achieve his freedom not through articulating his own needs but through subordinating himself to the Prince's need for service. For the servants, not all responsibility corresponds to freedom, but responsibility as regulated by time and purchased by wages, in so far as it frees them from continuous service to and thereby acknowledgment of social superiors, establishes the correspondence. Service according to an objective, regulative time schedule, as a force opposed to the subjective, whimsical demands for immediate gratification imposed by a master, works, in *1 Henry IV*, as a liberating force, and demarcates two kinds of servants according to their vision of freedom: one kind, such as the carrier, sees his freedom as getting to London before daybreak; the other kind, Francis, sees freedom as service to the Prince, or else revolt from the vintner in order to become an object of history, one of the "revolted tapsters, and ostlers trade-fall'n" (IV. ii. 29) who constitute Falstaff's "food for powder".

"MY STATE . . . SHOW'D LIKE A FEAST" *Hotspur and Henry*

History devours freedom: when the person governed by the immediate demands of appetite can delay those demands, he has developed a sense of time; when a person sees his own delayed demands within a sequence of other such demands and as potentially opposed to the demands and appetites of other people, he has developed a sense of history. Those unable to do so, those whose demands remain locked into the present or who see their delayed demands as either uninfluenced by or completely cor-respondent to the demands of others, have no freedom to act within history; they become the objects of history. Within the governing metaphor of *1 Henry IV*, those objectified by history become food.

Francis, or whatever group of Francises constitutes Falstaff's band of recruits, represents the most obvious instance in the play of a man's becoming the object of history. With the same naïvete with which Francis has believed he could attain a form of freedom by serving a more exalted master (the nostalgic freedom of service "not for meed", like Adam's in *As You Like It*), the "revolted tapsters, and ostlers trade-fall'n" seek freedom, from service or from trade, in military service to the state. In order to attain their ends, all offering service to the state must, to one degree or another, abstract and objectify other people; by their nature, politics and diplomacy, as demonstrated so clearly in the King's strategy session in this play, treat people like forces and objects. This requirement becomes most intense in military service, for in the military complete strangers who would be friendly or indifferent

to one another must absorb themselves in the requirements of
history and treat one another as mortal enemies. In military service
one must see one's self as a representative of history and must not
see an enemy as a person; thus, the soldier objectifies the enemy and
to a lesser extent objectifies himself as well. The lesser degree of
self-objectification normally enables the soldier to maintain a sense
of freedom or to see his service to the state as a way of eventually
asserting his freedom. One can objectify the enemy, and one's own
relation to the enemy, with relative ease in a war against a foreign
power, whose soldiers can be perceived as different, other, and
therefore as objects, thereby allowing the soldier to perceive
himself and his companions to the maximum degree as individual
persons, drawn together into a band of brothers. By the same
principle, one can only with difficulty objectify the enemy and
maintain subjectivity for one's self in a civil war, wherein on some
level the soldier feels a brotherhood and patriotic alliance with each
of his opponents.

King Henry tries to resolve this exact conflict at the outset of the
play, as he ostensibly wants to unite the English armies against a
remote, mysterious, and non-threatening foreign power:

> . . . Those opposed eyes,
> . . .
> Shall now, in mutual well-beseeming ranks,
> March all one way and be no more oppos'd
> Against acquaintance, kindred, and allies
> . . .
> Forthwith a power of English shall we levy,
> Whose arms were moulded in their mother's womb,
> To chase these pagans in those holy fields. (I. i. 9—24)

If he could establish such a sharp division between the state and its
enemies, there would be no forces that could turn back upon the
English soldiers and objectify and then devour them, and the
English state, which "did lately meet in the intestine shock / And
furious close of civil butchery" (12—13), would no longer devour
itself:

> No more the thirsty entrance of this soil
> Shall daub her lips with her own children's blood,
> No more shall trenching war channel her fields. (I. i. 5—7)

The King cannot, however, maintain the division between English
and foreign; domestic "broils" prevent the mounting of a crusade,
and the confluence of English rebels with Welsh and Scottish
invaders obliterates the distinction between native and alien
armies. When Prince Hal as Henry V brings a British (pointedly
not an English) army to France, the soldiers find personal
distinction and glory in military action, but in the battle at
Shrewsbury, which climaxes this play, no common soldiers
emerge from the masses. On the contrary: the play enunciates
throughout the battle the theme that even extraordinary soldiers
and personalities can be reduced into objects, specifically the
objects of appetite—food.

Before the battle Falstaff laughed that his recruits, whom he
already perceived as objects of his own appetite, would become
food for powder. At the end of the battle, Falstaff himself has
nearly become—Prince Hal thinks that he *has* become—"a fat
deer" (Hal had called Falstaff's recruits "rascals", which also means
young deer, *OED*, Definition 4), to be embowelled, powdered,
and eaten:

> Embowell'd! if thou embowel me to-day, I'll give you leave to
> powder me and eat me too tomorrow. (V. iv. 107, 111–13)

Hotspur charts a course similar to Falstaff's. He enters the battle
hoping "to tread on kings"; he ends as a part of the earth that is trod
upon. The Prince joins with Hotspur to pronounce the epitaph
that makes Hotspur the object of perhaps the lowest imaginable
form of appetite:

> Hotspur: . . . the earthy and cold hand of death
>   Lies on my tongue. No, Percy, thou art dust,
>   And food for . . .
> Prince: For worms, brave Percy. (V. iv. 84–6)

In short, during battle the soldier temporarily is reduced from an
individual with a history and an ego into the material object of
appetite; in war, the body becomes flesh. (After the battle, Hal
compliments Prince John of Lancaster for having "flesh'd / [his]
Maiden sword," 130–1.)

Henry IV, Part One, also activates the perception of the body as flesh away from the battlefield, which in part demonstrates that the military mentality pervades all phases of social and political life during civil war. The King and his rivals maintain, usurp, and relinquish power by seeing one another as food or, if as persons, as inactive subjects completely dependent on and controlled by appetite. King Henry claims to have seized the throne by making himself *appear* to be a "feast" (III. ii. 58), and he describes the reign of King Richard II in terms of induced nausea and surfeit: "being daily swallowed by men's eyes, / They surfeited with honey and began / To loathe the taste of sweetness", "being with his presence glutted, [gorg'd], and full", (70–3, 84). When the King thinks of punishing his rival Mortimer, he does so in terms of deprivation of food: "on the barren mountains let him starve" (I. iii. 89).[7] Worcester, in his challenge to and charge against the King, makes most clear the transformation through feeding from deprivation into assault:

> . . . Being fed by us you us'd us so
> As that ungentle gull, the cuckoo's bird,
> Useth the sparrow; did oppress our nest,
> Grew by our feeding to so great a bulk
> That even our love durst not come near your sight
> For fear of swallowing. (V. i. 59–64)

Those who see political actions as episodes of feeding, starvation, and oral attack project onto their world a vitality that otherwise could not exist. In this sense, King Henry, Worcester, and Falstaff, rather surprisingly, share a unified attitude: they each see the environment as sustaining, and man as dependent on the environment, requiring food to live and to grow, requiring public opinion and public support to advance in station.

Hotspur has the precisely opposite attitude. Hotspur sees the world as abstractions, which he in turn treats as objects. The obvious and extreme demonstration occurs during his address to "honour" which he would "pluck" (I. iii. 201–7). Hotspur sees the environment as dependent on his individual action—he wants to change the course of the river Trent in order to increase his share of the kingdom (III. i. 94–104)—and, correspondingly, he sees himself as independent of all public opinion and fellowship ("But out upon this half-fac'd fellowship!" (I. iii. 208). Hotspur completely disregards social propriety and its effect on others' attitudes, and thereby he aggravates the hostility between his family and the King's (by his impatient and neglectful refusal to release his prisoners (I. iii. 51-2), and he almost destroys the alliance of the rebels by his public rudeness and vulgarity (III. i.).[8] This same inattention to others makes Hotspur a perfect subject to be manipulated *by* others, as he is by Worcester, but Hotspur does not really care. So long as he remains free to act, he does not care in whose cause he acts: political concerns such as whose heirs should inherit the crown and if the kingdom should be divided do not concern *him*. In this sense Hotspur behaves like the consummate individualist, the man whose actions, as far as he can tell, have no ramifications.

It follows that although Hotspur has a sense of fame and of glory, he has no sense of history; he understands time, but not as a historical force. Hotspur's sense of time differs from Hal's as a stop watch does from a wrist watch. Hotspur, unlike the Prince, does not care to know the time of day or night—he rashly and impetuously wants to go to battle in the middle of the night (IV. iii.). For Hotspur, time merely imposes limits and boundaries, and forms a barrier between himself and battle: "O, let the hours be short, / Till fields, and blows, and groans applaud our sport!" (I. iii. 301-2). He equates time with "the time of life", and fails to see that one's life can affect future time. Hotspur's egocentric dying words summarize his severely limited comprehension of his place in history:

> life, time's fool,
> And time, that takes survey of all the world,
> Must have a stop. (V. iv. 81-3)

Hotspur equates the "loss of brittle life" (78) with the end of time. But time goes on after Hotspur dies; his failure to realize that life does not "ride upon a dial's point, / Still ending at the arrival of an hour" (V. ii. 83-4) makes his life meaningless to history. His whole life has been an accumulation of "glorious deeds" (III. ii. 146) and "proud titles" (V. iv. 79), of which, in death, he is "robb'd" (77), leaving him with nothing, or, put another way, leaving him as pure object, food for worms.

Hotspur's character, more unified and consistent than that of

any of the other protagonists, has neither the implicit con-
tradictions manifested by Falstaff nor the intentional duplicity and
ambivalence of the King and the Prince. This unified sensibility
characteristic of Hotspur has caused some readers to identify him
with the spirit of feudalism and to contrast Hotspur's sense of
power and obligation with the Lancastrian understanding and
employment of modern political methods. Other readers have
seen in Hotspur's implicit assumption that the throne belongs to
whomever is strong enough to seize it a version of the bourgeois
ethic of reward for individual action and merit, the mercantile
survival of the fittest,[9] in contrast with the (albeit politically
expedient) Lancastrian assumption that the crown should be
inherited and that subjects owe allegiance to the monarch. Both of
these attempts to determine what opposing world-views Hotspur
and the Prince represent derive from mistaken romantic notions
that identify feudalism with honour and with loyalty and from a
confused understanding of the hierarchical government of medieval England. We must remember that in medieval England the
King had not absolute but cumulative strength; he had authority
because he could call upon the feudal barons for military support.
The high nobility, the earls, in turn had power only to the extent
that they could call on the dukes, knights, and other retainers living
within their domain to supply military forces, as Hotspur's
strength in battle will depend on the "tenants, friends, and
neighboring gentlemen" that he "may have drawn together"
during the interval before the battle (III. i. 88–9). Each "level"
within the system had its authority determined by the amount of
force it could call upon from those below it and deliver to those
above. To describe the feudal system as pyramidal explains not its
shape but its structure, in that the height—the stature of any
individual member—depended on the strength of the base.

  The system of divine right, which the Prince and King invoke,
differs radically from the feudal system. The divine-right system
posits that subjects derive their strength from the King, and that
consequently one's stature increased in proportion to one's
proximity to the King. Power was not conceived of as structural
support but as radiation and emission; the dominant metaphor for
describing such a system shifts from the pyramid to the sun, a
metaphor flattering to and hence adopted by the monarch. The
analogy between the King giving forth power and God inspiring

the universe with life, when applied to the feudal system, transforms the static structure into an active process and further serves to locate power and authority at the apex of the pyramid or the centre of the system.

A metaphoric history of English politics might demonstrate a shift, between the fifteenth and seventeenth centuries, from one structure or system to the other, from the pyramid to the solar metaphor. J. W. Allen has argued, in fact, that the " 'theory of the divine right of Kings . . . was not formulated in England in the sixteenth century", that the theory "belongs to the seventeenth century".[10] The shift in metaphor, however, describes rather than creates the shift in political power and organization that occurred over the course of two centuries, between the time of Henry IV and Elizabeth. By Elizabeth's time, power had become increasingly centralized and therefore derived from the monarch, and the emergence of the divine-right metaphor late in Elizabeth's reign (Allen, p. 251) gave a literary manifestation to and expression of the current political conditions. In *1 Henry IV* Shakespeare examines not the conditions of the current, divine-right metaphors, but the origins of the metaphor, its emergence, as a part of a process, from the feudal/pyramidal system that during Shakespeare's lifetime it had begun to replace. The play superimposes the two metaphoric systems and creates dramatic conflict by treating the two systems as actual political forces in conflict. In other words, the play tries to discover the "location" of power in a literal sense: does the King have enough power to control his subjects or can the subjects combine forces to dethrone the King? Here a conflict develops between the dramatic and the metaphoric. The play shows that the King has greater military strength than, as well as a certain strategic advantage over, the rebel camp, in that one can more easily establish a system of military support than of alliance among diverse interests. The play then *uses* the King's military and tactical superiority to make it feel as though the modern, divine-right system that the King upholds must, by its nature, prevail over the feudal system he opposes. By identifying the modern world-view with the stronger side, Shakespeare makes us feel as though the divine-right system, in and of itself, is "good 'by nature' ".[11]

Hal, in conjunction with his metaphoric support of the divine-right theory, his identification of the King with the sun, speaks of power and of his intention to achieve power in decidedly modern, bourgeois terms. Aside from his fairly obvious commercial references—"redeeming time" and the more extended:

> Percy is but my factor, good my lord,
> To engross up glorious deeds on my behalf;
> And I will call him to so strict account
> That he shall render every glory up (III. ii. 147–50)

—the Prince also, in his soliloquy, speaks of power as a matter of relativism and perspective, in contrast to the traditional identification of degree of power with social position. The King and the King's only obvious peer and antagonist, Worcester, both of whom believe that only through strategy can one achieve power, express precisely the same views as does Hal. We can identify the modern attitude that these three characters share as an attempt to mediate violence, either to maintain or to replace the social system through rhetorical and political methods of persuasion, illusion, and deception and through accumulation of financial and capital resources, which represent the potential activation of military power. The Prince, King, and Worcester all use mediation—linguistic and symbolic actions—to actuate their political and military strategies. Hotspur, however, adopts the opposite, the medieval, view, which has nothing whatever to do with his sense either of loyalty to the King or of personal ambition. The medieval attitude, as enacted through Hotspur, opposes mediated violence, and brings about social change (note that the medieval attitude does not *oppose* social change) through the use of force.[12] In fact, Hotspur's insistence on the use of force and his failure to mediate force through rhetoric (when he would not relinquish his prisoners, the indications of his military success, to the King) dramatize his opposition to King Henry. The encounter Hotspur relates between himself and the King's messenger, who "demanded" the prisoners "in your Majesty's behalf" (I. iii. 47–8), presents a tableau depicting the opposition between mediated violence, expressed through rhetoric, style, costume, and manner, characteristic of the court, and immediate violence, the use of force and inattention to language, that characterizes Hotspur:

> When I was dry with rage and extreme toil,
> Breathless and faint, leaning upon my sword,
> Came there a certain lord, neat, and trimly dress'd,
> Fresh as a bridegroom, (I. iii. 31—4)

and, to emphasize the opposing views and uses of language:

> With many holiday and lady terms
> He questioned me, amongst the rest demanded
> My prisoners in your Majesty's behalf.
> I then, all smarting with my wounds being cold,
> To be so pest'red with a popinjay,
> Out of my grief and my impatience
> Answer'd neglectingly, I know not what—
> He should, or he should not. (I. iii. 46—53)

The episode is funny; the messenger reminds us of Osric, who carried to Hamlet Claudius's proposal of a duelling match between the Prince and Laertes. Just as the King's sending a fop such as Osric to propose a violent and treacherous encounter helps characterize the condition of Claudius's Danish court, King Henry's employment of this unnamed messenger as an ambassador to Hotspur emphasizes the King's conscious attempt to elevate himself above the use of force. The last act of the play dramatizes the breakdown of the King's rhetorical elevation, as his mediating agencies fail to perform their function of keeping the King removed from direct and violent encounter. The King admonishes Worcester that four members of the nobility:

> and many a creature else
> Had been alive this hour,
> If like a Christian thou hadst truly borne
> Betwixt our armies true intelligence; (V. v. 7—10)

the peace offering made by the King, words meant to prevent military encounter, was intentionally distorted in presentation so as to make violent encounter inevitable. Worcester superimposed his own mediating strategy on the King's; he used language to channel Hotspur's military strength away from the reconciliation that the King had proposed and into the service of his own political strategy. Similarly, the strategy of military mediation, the device of the "counterfeit", decoy kings, meant to protect the body of King Henry, served in part to ensure the death of those who "borrowed" the "title" of the King for the durance of the battle (V. iii. 22–4) and to increase the determination of Douglas, the King's eventual assailant.

The royal army achieves victory only when it abandons mediating strategies, and therefore the King's triumph results from his force, not from his rhetoric. Nothing in the play, including King Henry's own frank account of his rise to power, supports the King's claims that "thus ever did rebellion find rebuke", and "rebellion in this land shall lose his sway", (V. v. 1, 41). Rather, the confident tone of the conclusion reaffirms the King's earlier speculation about the significance of the foul, foreboding weather:

> King: How bloodily the sun begins to peer
> Above yon bulky hill! the day looks pale
> At his distemp'rature.
> Prince: The Southern wind
> Doth play the trumpet to his purposes,
> And by his hollow whistling in the leaves
> Foretells a tempest and a blust'ring day.
> King: Then with the losers let it sympathize,
> For nothing can seem foul to those that win. (V. i. 1–8)

Having won the battle by superior force, the King proclaims that the battle was won because rebellion is intrinsically, by its nature, wrong and therefore subject to defeat.

Because of Hotspur's limited perception of history and his dependence on immediate violence, he never could, either before or after battle, make a sophisticated claim to be fighting *for* what is right. Hotspur either fights in the service of his ego, to pluck honour and to accumulate glorious deeds, or else he fights so as to revenge his wounded vanity. Even when Hotspur raises the issue against which the King has the least defense—the issue of legitimate title—his antagonism toward Henry does not escape the closed circuit of his ego needs; he perceives Henry's dubious claim to title not as an injustice to Mortimer, but as a wound to his own pride (I. iii. 170–86). Hotspur and the rebel forces *could* have chosen to fight a battle of restoration, a struggle to return the throne to the most direct descendent of Richard II, Mortimer. Mortimer would then have received a portion of the divided kingdom had the rebel forces been victorious. But neither Hotspur nor any of his allies suggest that they are going to battle because the times are out of joint. In fact, both King Henry and Hotspur avoid the issue of legitimate title, but for precisely the opposite reasons. The King does so for pragmatic and political reasons (he has only a questionable claim to title, and therefore he does better to assert that he is a good king, not that he rightfully is or ought to be King), Hotspur does so for personal and temperamental reasons: he uses his perceptions about Henry's illegitimate title as an opportunity not for political restoration but for personal revenge and glory.

The issue of legitimate title, because in large part an issue of inheritance, extends outside the closed world of battle and adjoins, because it develops from, the world of domesticity and the family. Family life, however, has no place within Hotspur's limited vision of history. The family extends history through time and beyond the individual and his accomplishments; the family forms in a sense the environment of history, the continuation of property, title, and stature that only individual action—political, as with Henry IV; military, as with Hotspur himself—can oppose. Because Hotspur does not see time as extending beyond the individual and his actions ("time . . . must have a stop"), nor can he see the individual as extending beyond the immediate consequences of his actions (the victor wins the "proud titles" of the defeated, V. iv. 79), he works in opposition to the forces of historical continuity that the family, as the basis for legal inheritance, both creates and presupposes. In fact, Hotspur posits a diametric opposition between the qualities of war and the feminine, domestic qualities that he associates with the family. The language of the King's messenger, "with many holiday and lady terms", "so like a waiting-gentlewoman", (I. iii. 46, 55) exaggerates the disjunction between war, which for Hotspur constitutes history, and the family. As a consequence of Hotspur's divided attitude, while he prepares for the battle, his wife must be "banish'd" from his bed. Further, on the eve of the battle Hotspur treats his wife with deliberate and embarrassing coarseness, in part so as to effect a separation between himself and the simultaneous scene of marital affection and tenderness acted on stage by Lord and Lady Mortimer.

Hotspur's association of "holiday" with "lady terms" may have more than incidental significance; he makes a similar association later when berating his wife's language: "You swear like a comfit-maker's wife . . . Leave 'in sooth', /And such protest of pepper-gingerbread, /To velvet-guards and Sunday-citizens" (III. i. 247–56). Hotspur links ornamental language, femininity, and, perhaps, aspiration (in that his criticism of his wife contains a jab at the language of the middle classes) with the experience of holiday. Through his separation from his wife as well as from the messenger's heightened aestheticism and from the artistic (magical, poetic, and musical) performances that dominate the pre-battle conference, Hotspur attempts to establish a boundary between history and holiday, the one a world of individuality and action, the other of community and symbolic action.

Prince Hal becomes such a natural and obvious antagonist to Hotspur because, initially, he has just the opposite goal. By inverting the poles of holiday and everyday while in the tavern, claiming that his festive indulgence in Eastcheap works as a form of political calculation reluctantly undertaken, the Prince dissociates himself from the kinds of military glory and individual, public accomplishments through which Hotspur had become "the theme of honor's tongue" (I. i. 81). Instead, the Prince proposes a system of social relationships and symbolic actions by which he will redeem time and be more himself. We should not lose sight of the security about individual identity and social position that must precede and accompany a political strategy such as Prince Hal's; Hal, as I have mentioned, must always presume that or act as though he is Prince and heir apparent, and he must have confidence that the public has a predisposition to see the best in him once he "throws off" his "loose behavior". Here the differences in the political strategies adopted by the King and the Prince become significant, for, although both identify the presence of the King with the shining of the sun and both, further, believe that if the sun shines continuously people will become "with his presence glutted, [gorg'd], and full" (III. ii. 84), the King proposes the metaphor as a warning (against appearing too often to the public) whereas the Prince uses the metaphor as an opportunity within his strategic manipulation of public opinion.

The change in the strategic use of the sun /king metaphor, which shifts within one generation from cautionary to congratulatory

(King Henry speaks of how people grow tired of or from the sun; Prince Hal speaks of how people long for the sun), emphasizes the importance of inherited stature within the history play. Prince Hal, like the aristocratic comic protagonists, uses holiday retreat as a process that depends on his class status and that works to exaggerate and ensure the differentiation between himself and his social inferiors. As an event within a history play, however, Hal's retreat differs from the comic retreat primarily in that it does not return to a past state of things and does not re-establish a set of harmonious relations from the previous generation that the present generation has destroyed or jeopardized; on the contrary, Hal means his "holiday" as a direct assault on the values and traditions of the medieval political system. Yet in another way Hal's retreat asserts the importance, at least for Hal himself, of tradition, in that he can use the tavern environment and the strategy he devises therein as the alternative to the violent drive toward power, characteristic of Hotspur. The tavern strategy allows Hal the luxury of planning his future as if he ruled the kingdom by traditional rights of family inheritance, as if he need do nothing to secure those rights, as if he really needed popular support instead of either legitimate title or military predominance. Neither Hotspur nor the King can, like the Prince, resort to tradition as a guarantee of social stature; both must achieve or have achieved their stature through their own action, and consequently both must extirpate themselves from the familial world of domesticity and tradition in order to create a world of action and achievement antithetic to the world of languour and retreat.

In a sense, then, two different kinds of second worlds oppose the traditional world-view, the initial state of things, in the history play: the existing social order gets negated by the forces both of rebellion and of retreat. These two types of second worlds, however, function within the drama in radically different ways, and develop from totally different assumptions. The forces of rebellion, the social reorganization proposed by Bolingbroke in opposition to Richard, by Hotspur and Worcester in opposition to Henry, directly challenge the traditions of inheritence and primogeniture on which historic continuity is based. The process of holiday retreat, through which Prince Hal enacts his political strategy, seems to negate historical time, but actually works within historical time in a more subtle and more dependent way, for Hal could not initiate his symbolic actions without unshaken faith in the system of primogeniture, without personal confidence in his right to inherit the crown. Hal's second-world strategy, then, particularly in contrast with the actions of Worcester and Hotspur, both depends on and helps dramatize a conservative ideology: the apparent release from historical, or everyday, time and space actually allows the protagonist to project his own consciousness onto the material world, to organize and to perceive time and space so as to suit his psychological, and in this case also political, needs.

I began this section by stating rather bluntly that history devours freedom. This exact formula distinguishes the history play *1 Henry IV* from the comedies with which it is often compared. The history play, perhaps surprisingly, has less of a dialectical structure than the comedies, because the second world in the history play remains subordinate to historical time. In the comedies, the protagonists, because of their secure social stature, retain the freedom to negate primary-world time and space, to use time and space so as to create symbolically a world in their own image, out of their own subjective needs. In the history play, the protagonist, Prince Hal, also uses social stature to assert his supposed freedom from time, he also uses his subjective reorganization of time as a symbol for his control of the primary world. But the history play places this symbolic use of time in conjunction, and consequently in confrontation, with the objective world of historical time, a world whose process and pace the protagonist cannot control, a world that, in fact, questions the secure social stature on which the retreat to the second world depends. When historical time manifests itself in the second world, when "the sheriff with a most monstrous watch is at the door" (II. iv. 482–3) the protagonist must de-create the timeless antithetical world and must "to the court in the morning". In order to achieve his own place within history, Prince Hal must "be more himself" by acknowledging and submitting to the temporal forces that control the everyday world of the court and the battlefield.

The structure of the comedies depends on the fantasy that the regulating force of time does not apply equally to all social classes; the history play effectually dissolves both the structure and the fantasy, forcing Prince Hal to abandon his absolute control within the tavern for a qualified control, dependent on relative political and military strength, within the realm. During *1 Henry IV*, as the state and the rebels prepare for battle, the everyday/holiday opposition is negated and is replaced with the world of history, a world in which both the traditionally aristocratic appetite for continuous festivity and the temporal and spatial calculations and limitations of the bourgeois economy (the scrupulous parcelling out of public appearances, the calibrated division of the kingdom, the redeemed debt of time and of reputation) get displaced onto individual acts of heroic conflict. In the history play, the protagonists must abandon—or perhaps "banish"—the comic dialectic; the conflict shifts from an inconsequential opposition; between everyday time (Francis, the carriers) and timeless interlude (Falstaff, and initially Hal) to an opposition between individuals that gains significance entirely because of its consequences. Shakespeare's comedies end with a sense of closure—we hate to think of the eventual domestic consequences of the comic marriages—but his histories are "open-ended structures" (275).[13] The history plays, especially *1 Henry IV*, conclude with a conscious emphasis on the characters' awareness of uncompleted action. The last words of *1 Henry IV*—"Let us not leave till all our own be won" (V. iv. 44)—intentionally violate the expectation and anticipation of closure, and thereby emphasize the continuity between the historical time represented by the play and the historical time from within which an audience watches the play. We can distinguish *1 Henry IV* from the comedies because its protagonists achieve, incorporate, and then release to us a sense of the future.

Notes

CHAPTER 1 INTRODUCTION

1. S. Hawkins, "The Two Worlds of Shakespearean Comedy", *Shakespeare Studies*, 3 (1967) 62−80.
2. C. Leech, *"Twelfth Night" and Shakespearian Comedy* (Toronto: University of Toronto Press, 1965) p. 9.
3. H. Berger, Jr, "The Renaissance Imagination: Second World and Green World", *Centennial Review*, 9 (1965) 36−78.
4. S. Freud, *Introductory Lectures on Psycho-Analysis* (1916−1917, 1915−1917), James Strachey (ed. and trans.), *The Standard Edition of the Complete Psychological Works*, XVI (London: The Hogarth Press and the Institute for Psycho-Analysis, 1963) p. 417.

CHAPTER 2 THE MERCHANT OF VENICE

1. T. Bright, *Treatise of Melancholy* (1586), quoted in John Russell, Brown (ed.), *The Merchant of Venice: The Arden Edition*, rev. ed. (1959; rpt. New York: Random House, 1964), p. 129n.
2. Another object that correlates to subjective social and economic values in *The Merchant* is the casket. In Venice a casket stores and conveys material wealth, whereas in Belmont the material value of the casket is subordinate to its value as a representative, ceremonial token. Since the same casket is not used in Venice and Belmont, even though the same stage prop may be used to *represent* the different caskets, the casket is not as precise an objective symbol as is the ring.
3. Shylock also experiences the contradiction between the exchange and the ceremonial value of a ring; he is tortured because the ring given him by Leah when he was a bachelor has been exchanged, by his daughter, "for a monkey" (III. i. 118−22).
4. Antonio's requesting Bassanio to give up the ring is Shakespeare's addition to the source material, K. Muir, *Shakespeare's Sources, Comedies and Tragedies*, I (London: Methuen, 1961) p. 51.
5. C. L. Barber *Shakespeare's Festive Comedy* (1959; rpt. Cleveland: World Publishing Co., 1963), p. 170. There are many variations on the theme that money is only valuable either in regard to the way it is used or as a symbol of love or of generosity, that life must come before money. See especially G. W. Knight, "The Ideal Production" *Principles of Shakespearian Production*, rpt. in *Twentieth-Century Interpretations of The Merchant of Venice*, S. Barnet, (ed.) (Englewood Cliffs, New Jersey: Prentice-Hall, 1970), pp. 92−3; Thomas Marc Parrott, *Shakespearean Comedy* (New York: Russell and Russell, 1949), p. 143;

J. R. Brown, *Shakespeare and His Comedies*, 2nd ed. (1962; rpt. London: Methuen, 1968), pp. 61—75; S. Barnet, "Introduction" in *Twentieth-Century Interpretations*, Barnet (ed.), pp. 3—4; T. Weiss, *The Breath of Clowns and Kings* (New York: Atheneun, 1971), p. 153; A. Hobson, *Full Circle* (London: Chatto and Windus, 1972), p. 207; and A. Barton, "Introduction" to *The Merchant of Venice*, G. B. Evans (ed.), *The Riverside Shakespeare* (Boston: Houghton Mifflin (1974) pp. 251—2.

6. Heine, *Sämmtliche Werke*, V (Philadelphia, 1856) p. 324, quoted in *The Merchant of Venice: A New Variorum Edition*, H. H. Furness (ed.), (Philadelphia: J. B. Lippincott, 1888) pp. 450—1.

7. The only interpretation of *The Merchant* as completely and consistently ironic is developed by A. D. Moody, *Shakespeare: The Merchant of Venice*, Studies in English Literature, No. 21 (Woodbury, New York: Barron's, 1964). Since I agree with so many of Moody's readings of specific passages in *The Merchant*, and with his refutation of so many previous critics, I think it is especially important to emphasize the fundamental differences between our conclusions about this play and, by doing so, to distinguish between dialectical and ironic criticism.

8. F. Jameson, *Marxism and Form* (Princeton, New Jersey: Princeton University Press, 1971) pp. 328—9.

9. S. Barnet, "Prodigality and Time in *The Merchant of Venice*", *PMLA*, 87 (1972) 26—30, points out that "Shylock sells time, whereas Bassanio, given to leisure and entertainment, is prodigal with time" (29). Barnet does not identify these opposed attitudes with the ideologies of opposed social classes.

10. M. Van Doren, *Shakespeare* (1939; rpt. Garden City, New York: Doubleday, n.d.) p. 84.

CHAPTER 3   A MIDSUMMER NIGHT'S DREAM

1. R. Girard's discussion of "mediated desire" in his *Violence and the Sacred*, P. Gregory (tr.) (1972; rpt. Baltimore, Maryland: The Johns Hopkins University Press, 1977), has influenced my thinking here about the Athenian lovers.

2. R. W. Dent, "Imagination in *A Midsummer Night's Dream*", *Shakespeare Quarterly*, 15 (1964) 115—29.

3. H. Nemerov, "The Marriage of Theseus and Hippolyta", *Kenyon Review*, 18 (1956) 633—41.

4. C. L. Barber, op. cit.

5. A complete annotation of this statement would read, I am afraid, much like a bibliography for *A Midsummer Night's Dream*. The major critics, exclusive of those whom I disciss separately below, who describe the conclusion of the play with the terms I have cited include:

(i) *Harmony*. G. W. Knight, *The Shakespearian Tempest*, 3rd ed. (1932; rpt. London: Methuen, 1953); N. Coghill, *Shakespeare's Professional Skills* (Cambridge: Cambridge University Press, 1964) p. 40.

(ii) *Concord*. L. Guilhamet, "*A Midsummer-Night's Dream* as the Imitation of an Action", *SEL*, 15 (1975) 257—71.

(iii) *Variety* or *Comprehensiveness*. H. B. Charlton, *Shakespearian Comedy* (1938; rpt. New York: Barnes and Noble, n.d.), p. 120; M. Mincoff,

"Shakespeare and Lyly", *Shakespeare Survey*, 14 (1961) 15–24; G. Wickham, *Shakespeare's Dramatic Heritage* (London: Routledge and Kegan Paul, 1969), p. 189; I. Ribner, "Introduction" to *A Midsummer Night's Dream* in Ribner and G. L. Kitteredge (eds.), *Complete Works of Shakespeare* (Lexington, Massachusetts: Xerox College Publishing, 1971) p. 219.

(iv) *Balance* or *Pluralism* W. Clemen, "Introduction" to *A Midsummer Night's Dream* (1963) in S. Barnet (gen. ed.), *Complete Signet Classic Shakespeare* (New York: Harcourt Brace, 1972) pp. 524–5), 528; D. P. Young, *Something of Great Constancy* (New Haven: Yale University Press, 1966) *passim*, but especially: the "consistently comic" artist "balances opposing values and forces in a way that allows us to commit ourselves to neither", (p. 114); R. Cody, *The Landscape of the Mind* (Oxford: Clarendon Press, 1969) pp. 132, 144–6; R. F. Miller, "*A Midsummer Night's Dream*: The Fairies, Bottom, and the Mystery of Things", *Shakespeare Quarterly*, 26 (1975) 254–68.

(v) *Reconciled Contrast* Enid Welsford, *The Court Masque* (1927; rpt. New York: Russell and Russell, 1962) p. 338; Nemerov, "Marriage", 640–1; P. G. Phialas, *Shakespeare's Romantic Comedies* (Chapel Hill: University of North Carolina Press, 1966) esp. p. 130; R. A. Zimbardo, "Regeneration and Reconciliation in *A Midsummer Night's Dream*", *Shakespeare Studies*, 6 (1972) 35–50; A. Barton, "Introduction" to *A Midsummer Night's Dream*, in G. B. Evans (ed.), *The Riverside Shakespeare* (Boston: Houghton Mifflin, 1974) p. 218.

6. P. F. Fisher, "The Argument of *A Midsummer Night's Dream*", *Shakespeare Quarterly*, 8 (1957) 307–10.
7. G. K. Hunter, *Shakespeare: The Later Comedies*, Writers and Their Work, No. 143 (London: Longmans, Green, 1962) pp. 7–20. For other writers who argue that *A Midsummer Night's Dream* fulfils a dance-like pattern see Welsford, pp. 331, 334; T. W. Baldwin, *On the Literary Genetics of Shakespeare's Plays, 1592–1954* (Urbana: University of Illinois Press, 1959) pp. 472–92; Francis Fergusson, *Shakespeare: The Pattern in His Carpet* (New York: Dell Publishing Co., 1971) p. 123.
8. B. O. Bonazza, *Shakespeare's Early Comedies* (The Hague: Mouton, 1966), p. 123.
9. J. E. Robinson, "The Ritual and Rhetoric of *A Midsummer Night's Dream*", *PMLA*, 83 (1968) 380–91.
10. C. L. Barber, op. cit. p. 159.
11. S. P. Zitner, "The Worlds of *A Midsummer Night's Dream*", *South Atlantic Quarterly*, 59 (1960), 397–403.

CHAPTER 4 AS YOU LIKE IT

1. J. Shaw, "Fortune and Nature in *As You Like It*", *Shakespeare Quarterly*, 6 (1955) 45–50.
2. A. O. Lovejoy and G. Boas, *Primitivism and Related Ideas in Antiquity* (1935; rpt. New York: Octagon Books, 1965), Appendix: "Some Meanings of 'Nature'", pp. 447–56. The authors cite 66 definitions of "nature". References to their definitions, identified by number, in the text.

3. J. R. Brown, *Shakespeare and His Comedies*, 2nd ed. (1962; rpt. London: Methuen, 1968) p. 149.

4. S. Freud, "Psycho-Analytic Notes on an Autobiographical Account of a Case of Paranoia (Dementia Paranoides) (1911–12)", Alice and James Strachey (trans.), in *Standard Edition of the Complete Psychological Works* XII, James Strachey (ed.), (London: The Hogarth Press and the Institute of Psycho-analysis, 1957) pp. 63, 71.

5. R. Pierce, "The Moral Language of *Rosalynde* and *As You Like It*", *Studies in Philology*, 68 (1971) 167–176; M. M. Schwartz, *A Thematic Introduction to Shakespeare* (Saratoga Springs, New York: Empire State College, 1974) p. 44; J. Swan, "History, Pastoral and Desire: A Psychoanalytic Study of English Renaissance Literature and Society", (Diss. Stanford 1974) pp. 240–1.

6. A. H. Tolman, "Shakespeare's Manipulation of his Sources in *As You Like It*", *Modern Language Notes*, 37 (1922) 65–76, observed that, in *Rosalynde*, Rosalyne (Rosalind) urges Rosader (Orlando) to woo Aliena (Celia/Aliena), and thereby tests his faith, 69–70.

7. S. Freud, op. cit., p. 63.

8. D. J. Palmer, "Art and Nature in *As You Like It*", *Philological Quarterly*, 49 (1970) 30–40.

9. A. R. Cirillo, "*As You Like It*: Pastoralism Gone Awry", *ELH*, 38 (1971) 19–39.

10. W. Empson, *Some Versions of Pastoral* (N.d.; rpt. New York: New Directions, 1960) p. 27.

11. See, for example, Lodge's *Rosalynde*:

> By my faith (quoth Aliena [Celia]) sir, you are deepe read in love, or growes your insight into affection by experience? . . . But sir our countrey amours are not like your courtly fancies, nor is our wooing like your suing: for poore shepheards never plaine them till Love paine them, where the Courtiers eyes is full of passions when his heart is most free from affection: . . .

Rpt. in H. H. Furness (ed.), *New Variorum Edition of "As You Like It"* (1890; rpt. New York: Dover Publications, 1963) p. 371.

12. R. Poggioli, "The Oaten Flute", *Harvard Library Bulletin*, 11 (1957) 147–184.

13. The phrases in quotations are the titles of two recent books on the pastoral: R. Cody, *The Landscape of the Mind* (Oxford: Clarendon Press, 1969) and D. Young, *The Heart's Forest* (New Haven: Yale University Press, 1972). Both books treat the pastoral environment as a product or a consequence of the protagonists' subjectivity.

14. J. Hasler, *Shakespeare's Theatrical Notation: The Comedies* (Bern: Francke Verlag, 1974) p. 199.

15. L. Lerner, *The Uses of Nostalgia* (London: Chatto and Windus, 1972) p. 118.

16. H. E. Toliver, *Pastoral Forms and Attitudes* (Berkeley: University of California Press, 1971) pp. 111, 114.

CHAPTER 5 TWELFTH NIGHT

1. C. L. Barber, *Shakespeare's Festive Comedy* (rpt. Cleveland: World Publishing Co., 1963).

2. J. Hollander, *"Twelfth Night* and the Morality of Indulgence", in *Sewanee Review*, 68, No. 2 rpt. in Alvin B. Kernan (ed.), *Modern Shakespeare Criticism*, (New York: Harcourt, Brace and World, 1970) pp. 228–241.

3. M. P. Tilley, "The Organic Unity of *Twelfth Night*", *PMLA*, 29 (1914) 550–66.

4. J. Hasler, *Shakespeare's Theatrical Notation: The Comedies* (Bern: Francke Verlag, 1974) p. 161.

5. E. Welsford, *The Fool* (London: Faber and Faber, 1935) p. 248.

6. The Duke's servants in *Gl'Ingannati*, one of the sources for *Twelfth Night*, detest the newly arrived servant, Lelia, whose part is analogous to Viola's. "He hath robbed me of my place", one complains, II. vi. See G. Bullough (ed.), *Narrative and Dramatic Sources of Shakespeare*, II (London: Routledge and Kegan Paul, 1958) p. 309.

7. The context forces me to be unduly cursory in my discussion of bourgeois and Puritan characteristics. My discussion refers only the received ideas, in their broad outline, associated with these economic and religious movements. The connection between Puritanism and the bourgeois virtues is discussed in great detail in R. H. Tawney, *Religion and the Rise of Capitalism* (New York: Harcourt, 1926) and Christopher Hill, *Puritanism and Revolution* (London: Martin Secker and Warburg, 1958); *The Century of Revolution* (London: Thomas Nelson, 1961); *Society and Puritanism in Pre-Revolutionary England* (New York: Schocken, 1964); *Intellectual Origins of the English Revolution* (Oxford: Clarendon, 1965); *Reformation to Industrial Revolution*, The Pelican Economic History of Britain, II (Harmondsworth: Pelican Books, 1969); and *The World Turned Upside Down* (1972; rpt. Harmondsworth: Penguin Books, 1975).

8. O. J. Campbell, *Shakespeare's Satire* (1943; rpt. Hampden, Connecticut: Archon Books, 1963), p. 87. Campbell's argument that Malvolio represents a threat to the aristocrats because he emphasizes that they will have to economize, change their ways, in order to survive as a class, anticipates the work of Lawrence Stone, *The Crisis of the Aristocracy* (Oxford: Clarendon, 1965). Stone of course challenged R. H. Tawney's long-held view that the aristocracy primarily feared displacement by a rising bourgeoisie (see *Religion and the Rise of Capitalism*). J. W. Draper, "Olivia's Household", *PMLA*, 49 (1934) 797–806, and M. Van Doren, *Shakespeare* (1939; rpt. Garden City, New York: Doubleday, n.d.), applied Tawney's view to *Twelfth Night*, arguing that Malvolio has "offended" the aristocracy "as a class", (Van Doren, p. 140).

9. P. G. Phialas, *Shakespeare's Romantic Comedies* (Chapel Hill: The University of North Carolina Press, 1966) p. 270. See also H. Jenkins, "Shakespeare's *Twelfth Night*", *Rice Institute Pamphlet*, 45 (1959), rpt. in *Shakespeare: The Comedies*, K. Muir (ed.) (Englewood Cliffs, New Jersey: Prentice-Hall, 1965) p. 73; L. S. Champion, *The Evolution of Shakespeare's Comedies* (Cambridge, Massachusetts: Harvard University Press, 1970) p. 94; and Theodore Wiess, *The Breath of Clowns and Kings* (New York: Atheneum, 1971) p. 306, all of whom

argue that *Twelfth Night*—or, more specifically, Viola—educates Orsino and Olivia.

10. J. Markes, "Shakespeare's Confluence of Tragedy and Comedy: *Twelfth Night* and *King Lear*", *Shakespeare Quarterly*, 15, No. 2 (1964) 75—88. Page references given in parentheses.
11. C. Dennis, "The Vision of *Twelfth Night*", *Tennessee Studies in Literature*, 18 (1973) 63—74.
12. B. S. Field, Jr, "Fate, Fortune, and *Twelfth Night*", *Michigan Academician*, 6 (1973) 193—9.
13. A. Leggatt, *Shakespeare's Comedy of Love* (London: Methuen, 1974) pp. 252—3.
14. L. G. Salingar, "The Design of *Twelfth Night*", *Shakespeare Quarterly*, 9 (1958) 117—39.
15. F. B. Tromly, "*Twelfth Night*: Folly's Talents and the Ethics of Shakespearean Comedy", *Mosaic*, 7, No. 3 (1974) 53—68.
16. Joan Hartwig, "Feste's 'Whirligig' and the Comic Providence of *Twelfth Night*", *ELH*, 40 (1973) 501—13.

CHAPTER 6 HENRY IV, PART ONE

1. R. Battenhouse, "Falstaff as Parodist and Perhaps Holy Fool", *PMLA*, 90 (1975) 32—52.
2. M. D. Faber, "Falstaff Behind the Arras", *American Imago*, 27 (1970) 197—225.
3. C. L. Barber, *Shakespeare's Festive Comedy* (1959; rpt. Cleveland: World Publishing Co., 1963), argues that "the holiday-everyday antithesis is [Hal's] resource for control" (p. 196) and "the misrule works, through the whole dramatic rhythm, to consolidate rule", (p. 205).
4. A familiar argument, raised by E. M. W. Tillyard, *Shakespeare's History Plays* (1946; rpt. New York: Barnes and Noble, 1964) p. 274; Jonas A. Barish, "The Turning Away of Prince Hal", *Shakespeare Studies*, 1 (1965), rpt. in R. J. Dorius (ed.) *Twentieth-Century Interpretations of "Henry IV, Part One"*, (Englewood Cliffs, New Jersey: Prentice-Hall, 1970) pp. 83—8.

When he sounds the base string of humility in the company of the drawers, Hal is putting himself in vital touch with the whole spectrum of English life; (p. 85)

I. Ribner, *The English History Play in the Age of Shakespeare*, rev. ed. (London: Methuen, 1965):

[Hal] learns to know the common people who will be perhaps his most powerful allies when he attains the crown; (p. 173)

E. Sjöberg, "From Madcap Prince to King: The Evolution of Prince Hal", *Shakespeare Quarterly*, 20 (1969) 11—16; A. C. Dessen, "The Intemperate Knight and the Politic Prince: Late Morality Structure in *1 Henry IV*", *Shakespeare Studies*, 7 (1974) 147—71; and the Marxist critic William B. Stone,

"Literature and Class Ideology: *Henry IV, Part One*", *College English*, 33 (1972) 891–900.

5. E. M. W. Tillyard, op. cit., pp. 276–7.
6. S. P. Zitner, "Anon, Anon: or, a Mirror for a Magistrate", *Shakespeare Quarterly*, 19 (1968) 63–70.
7. The *Oxford English Dictionary* cites this passage as one of the first instances of Definition 4 of *starve*: "to die of hunger".
8. T. D. Bowman, "Two Addenda to Hotspur's Tragic Behavior", *Journal of General Education*, 16 (1964) 68–71, and Judith C. Levinson, "'Tis a Woman's Fault'", *ELN*, 11 (1973) 38–40, discuss Hotspur's vulgar behaviour during the conference with Glendower.
9. More critics have argued that Hotspur embodies feudalism. See D. Traversi, *Shakespeare from "Richard II" to "Henry IV"*, (Stanford, California: Stanford University Press, 1957) p. 89; Barber, op. cit. pp. 202–3; A. La Branche, "'If Thou Wert Sensible of Courtesy': Private and Public Virtue in *Henry IV, Part One*", *Shakespeare Quarterly*, 17 (1966) 379; C. Barber, "Prince Hal, Henry V, and the Tudor Monarchy", in D. W. Jefferson (ed.) *The Morality of Art*, (London: Routledge and Kegan Paul, 1969) p. 68; and F. Bowers, "Theme and Structure in *King Henry IV, Part 1*", in *The Drama of the Renaissance*, E. M. Blistein (ed.) (Providence, Rhode Island: Brown University Press, 1970) pp. 67–68. For the opposing view, that Hotspur represents the "New Man", see J. F. Danby, *Shakespeare's Doctrine of Nature* (London: Faber and Faber, 1949) p. 88, and A. B. Kernan, "The Henriad: Shakespeare's Major History Plays," in Kernan (ed.), *Modern Shakespearean Criticism*, (New York: Harcourt, Brace and World, 1970):

> Honour, as Hotspur understands it, is . . . the Renaissance thirst for individual fame, for immortality of reputation. (p. 258)

10. J. W. Allen, *A History of Political Thought in the Sixteenth Century* (1928; rpt. London: Methuen, 1961) pp. 268–270.
11. Arthur O. Lovejoy and George Boas, op. cit., cite as definition Definition 45 of *nature*:

> Good 'by nature' is that social order in which political power coincides with 'natural' power, i.e., in which the stronger rule. (p. 452)

See, for additional discussion of Lovejoy and Boas's definitions, above, pp. 112–17, 140–1.
12. Lawrence Stone, *The Crisis of the Aristocracy* (Oxford: The Clarendon Press, 1965) pp. 239–42, discusses the opposition between the sixteenth-century English central government that mediated and litigated conflict and the medieval English aristocracy, dependent on personal violence for resolution of conflict among the nobility.
13. David Scott Kastan, "The Shape of Time: Form and Value in the Shakespearean History Play", *Comparative Drama*, 7 (1973) 259–77.

Index